The Power of the AC Electrics

1.
 Resplendent in InterCity Sector livery of light and dark grey with red band, Class 87/0 Bo-Bo No .87010 *King Arthur* approaches Euston station on 10th April 1986 with the 09.30 express from Liverpool Lime Street, which has made scheduled stops at Runcorn, Crewe and Stafford along the way.

2.
Before the advent of the M6 Motorway, the only sound, apart from passing trains, that could be heard from this vantage point in the Lune Gorge, near Tebay, was the cry of the curlew! On 3rd June 1977, Class 86/2 No. 86239 makes light of the Cumbrian gradients and speeds through the countryside with the 16.15 express from Liverpool Lime Street to Glasgow Central. In November 1980 this locomotive received the name *L.S. Lowry*.

The Power of the AC Electrics

Brian Morrison

Oxford Publishing Co.

Published by:
Haynes Publishing Group
Sparkford, Near Yeovil, Somerset. BA22 7JJ

Haynes Publications Inc.
861 Lawrence Drive, Newbury Park, California 91320, USA.

Morrison, Brian.
  The power of the AC electrics.
  1. Great Britain. Railway Services. British Rail.
  Electric locomotives, to 1988.
  I. Title.
  625.2'63' 0941

  ISBN 0-86093-246-X

Library of Congress catalog card number
88-82511

3.
Glinting under a late autumn sun, Class 83 No. 83012 passes Willesden on 21st October 1984 with a haul of empty coaching stock from an earlier arrival at Euston station.

Brian Beer

Introduction

This final volume of the modern traction Power series has been something of a stop-go project since the publication was first envisaged over eight years ago. The album was originally intended to be published before other companion volumes describing the Classes 31 and 33, but the great number of changes that took place within British Rail's fleet of AC electric locomotives, coupled with the appearance of the third generation types 89, 90 and 91 necessitated many changes and revisions to the initial project. In consequence, this pictorial history of BR's main line AC electric fleet is right up to date with the inclusion of all recent developments.

The album deals individually with each type from Class 81 through to 91 and detailed drawings from the expert hand of Russell Carter are a feature throughout. Each type is shown pictorially from the year of introduction to the present day, their sphere of operation is acknowledged within the context of the photographs displayed, and the various changes that have come about to external appearances are fully documented.

Well over 250 photographs are contained in the album in order to illustrate all aspects of operations and, in this respect, thanks go to the darkroom mastery of Derek Mercer who undertook the printing of the majority of the negatives. Thanks also go to the many photographers who willingly made their collections available for the project, particularly

Colin Marsden whose archive collection, together with his own photographs have been invaluable. Finally, a thank you to Mike Scott of GEC, Allan Baker of Stratford Major Depot and Stephen Ford of BREL for the assistance they have readily given in providing both information and facilities for taking a number of the photographs.

Brian Morrison
Sidcup, Kent

All photographs are by the author unless stated otherwise and all drawings are by Russell Carter.

Bibliography

100 Years of Electric Traction
Colin J. Marsden (Oxford Publishing Company)
AC Electric Locomotives of British Rail
Brian Webb & John Duncan (David & Charles)
The Allocation History of BR Diesels & Electrics
Roger Harris (Roger Harris)
British Rail Fleet Survey – Electric Locomotives
Brian Haresnape (Ian Allan)
British Rail Motive Power
Roger Wood (Ian Allan)
Electric Locomotives on the West Coast Main Line
Roly Longhurst & Michael Oakley (D. Bradford Barton)

4.
Passing the stretch of line where Bushey water troughs were situated in steam days, Class 81 No. 81009 heads northwards with a Freightliner from Willesden FLT on 30th June 1976.

Prototype

The first AC electric locomotive to run on BR metals was not No. E3001, of what was to become Class 81, in Autumn 1959 but a converted Western Region gas turbine locomotive in the Autumn of 1958. With authorisation for electrification of the London Midland Region's main line from Euston, and the subsequent placement of orders with various manufacturers for 100 AC electric locomotives, crew training and line testing prior to their initial introduction some twelve months hence was desirable, and the former WR gas turbine No. 18100 was utilised in the interim. The conversion of a 130 ton gas turbine to a 105 ton AC electric was undertaken at the Stockton-on-Tees works of Metropolitan-Vickers/Beyer Peacock Ltd between January and October of 1958. During this period the considerable alterations involved, included among other

things, the removal of the gas turbine unit and combustion chambers with associated DC electric generating equipment, together with the fuel tanks, control gear and filtering units. Also, conversion of the driving cabs from left to right-hand drive with all instrumentation conforming to the agreed design for the new AC locomotives, and lowering part of the roof between the cabs to allow for the required fitting of the pantograph head and other roof equipment within the loading gauge. First re-numbered E1000 and later E2001, the black and silver liveried machine was initially set to work on the first electrified section of the Crewe-Manchester route, the Styal line, between Wilmslow and Mauldeth Road and later spent time at Allerton and Crewe depots and in Glasgow prior to withdrawal in 1968.

5

Constructed as a gas turbine by Metropolitan-Vickers in 1951, No. 18100 was withdrawn from service in January 1958 but survived as British Rail's prototype AC electric locomotive until withdrawn for the second time ten years later. It finally met its end at the breakers Cashmores of Tipton during January 1973.

Colin J. Marsden collection

6.

Above: Apart from the Stone-Faiveley pantograph and roof equipment, the external differences between the original Western Region gas turbine and the 'new' AC electric No. E1000 were remarkably few and far between; the locomotive even retaining its original livery and nickname of ''Black Bess''. The buffers are not damaged as they may appear to be, but have had a slice cut from each to allow for a less-generous London Midland Region loading gauge at platform level.

Colin J. Marsden collection

7.

Below: Carrying the final number of E2001, British Rail's first 25kV AC electric locomotive is tested inside the Rugby Test Station on 7th April 1963.

Colin J. Marsden collection

Drawing A.
Type AL1 No. E3001 as originally constructed and showing two pantographs – 'B' side.

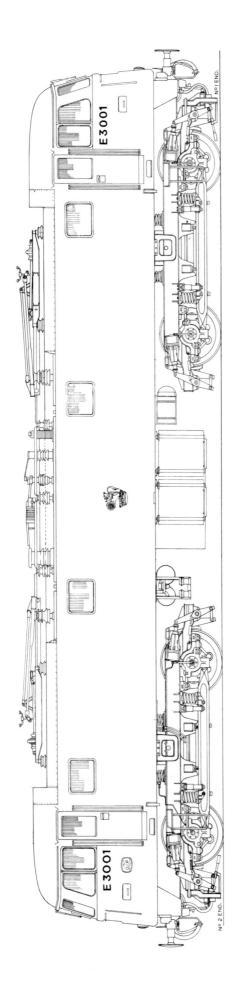

Drawing B.
Class 81 No. 81001 as modified in 1978 – 'A' side.

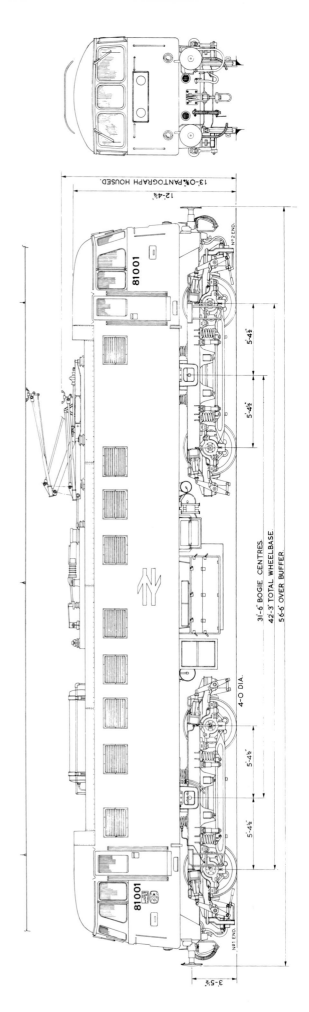

Class 81 (AL1)

British Railway's electrification of the Crewe-Manchester/Liverpool routes at 25kV AC brought about a new era in railway modernisation. The modest beginning in 1959 grew into the largest ever transformation of Britain's railway system, culminating in electrically-hauled services from Euston to Glasgow, Liverpool Street to Cambridge and Norwich, and King's Cross to Edinburgh at unprecedented average speeds. For the initial fleet of locomotives for the West Coast Main Line, 100 examples were ordered from five different manufacturers, with 60 emanating from private industry and 40 from BR's own workshops. Twenty of the initial order were to be for locomotives with lower gear ratios for hauling heavy freight loads but, in the final analysis, this was found unnecessary and the five that were so constructed were later modified to standard.

The manufacturers were given quite a lot of individual freedom with the electrical designs but were required to follow specification for an 80 ton Bo-Bo mixed traffic locomotive with driving controls to be similar in all cases, and based upon the BTC Design Panel's concepts of appearance.

The order for 23 AL1s, as they were known prior to the TOPS re-numbering scheme, was given to Associated Electrical Industries (AEI), who subcontracted the mechanical construction to the Birmingham Railway Carriage & Wagon Company (BRC&W). The first completed locomotive was handed over to the British Transport Commission at Sandbach station in November 1959 and carried No. E3001.

8.
Constructed at the Smethwick works of BRC&W in June 1961, Class AL1 No. E3021 (now 81018) shows off the attractive 'electric blue' livery with white roof and cab surrounds and raised aluminium casting of number and BR 'lion and wheel' totem as received by all the pilot scheme electric locomotives from new. The roof, in fact, was made of fibre glass but the cabs were steel.

Colin J. Marsden collection

9.
The first of the 100 prototype AC electric locomotives to be delivered was No. E3001, which commenced driver training and testing runs in December 1959. It is shown here at that time with a test train on the Styal line. The two bodywork sides were completely different; the side shown here having nine louvered air-intake grilles, while the other side displayed four windows as illustrated opposite. All were originally constructed with two Stone-Faiveley pantographs but this was found to be unnecessary and one was later removed. As No. 81001 this locomotive caught fire on 26th August 1983 while hauling the Euston-Stirling Motorail near Carstairs and was subsequently withdrawn from service. It was held in store at Crewe Works for over three years and finally cut up there in September 1986.

Colin J. Marsden collection

10.
The old and new orders at Watford Junction in October 1965. Heading southwards, Class AL1 No. E3005 (now 81004) hauls an unfitted ballast train complete with two brake vans.

C.R. Lewis Coles

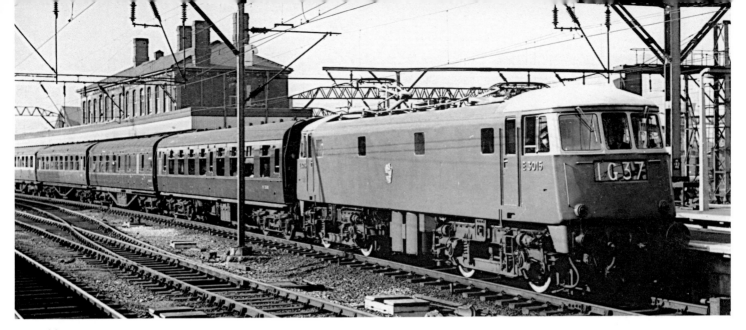

11.
No. E3015 (now 81013) glides away from Stockport in the early 1960s hauling all-maroon stock. Apart from the differing bodywork on the two sides, it can be observed here that the underslung equipment is also dissimilar, the side with the windows originally having two smoothing chokes projecting downwards, providing natural air-convection for cooling the motors.

Norman E. Preedy

12.
At the buffer stops of Liverpool Lime Street station on 25th June 1964, No. E3008 (now 81007) has arrived with an express from Euston. Apart from the forerunner of the class, No. E3001 (81001), none of the other Class 81 TOPS computer numbers co-incided with the last two digits of the original ones as, when the change came about, three of the fleet, (Nos E3002, E3009 and E3019), had been previously withdrawn as a result of fire or accident damage, and another two, (Nos E3096 and E3097), were originally numbered out of sequence into the series reserved for the heavy freight haulage types.

C.R. Lewis Coles

13.
A small two-road maintenance building serving Manchester Longsight's newly acquired electric locomotives was constructed in 1960 alongside what was then known as South shed; the remaining steam traction being banished to North shed. Before the floors were allowed to become tarnished by use, two Class AL1s pose inside the building for an official photograph.

Colin J. Marsden collection

14.
Liverpool's Allerton depot, between Runcorn and Lime Street stations, is responsible for maintenance and availability of diesel and electric main line and shunting power for the whole of the area. In this early 1960's view, four Class AL1s, from left to right Nos E3005, E3006, E3004 and E3010, are lined up for the official camera.

Colin J. Marsden collection

15.
The year 1966 saw the beginning of the end for the attractive light blue paintwork applied to the AC electric locomotives. BR decreed that, in accordance with their new 'corporate image', all motive power was required to have new blue livery with full-yellow ends and to display BR's newly designed symbol, thus requiring removal of the distinctive raised aluminium 'lion and wheel'. Now with just the one pantograph, No. E3096 (numbered 81021 until withdrawn in April 1987) takes the 14.00 Dagenham-Garston, Silcock & Collings Group 'cartic' train past Willesden yards, on the approach to Wembley Central, on 26th June 1972. One of the two Class AL1s originally constructed for haulage of heavy freight loads, this locomotive carried number E3301 prior to standard conversion.

16.
With a metal plate and marker lights fitted in place of the obsolete route indicator panel, No. 81008 races through Bushey & Oxhey station on 29th April 1978 with an eleven-coach ADEX special train for Euston. The original raised numbers, E3010, have been removed and the new number painted in. Happily the new BR symbol, however, is still of the raised variety although now made in metal alloy. In March 1988 No. 81003 was finally withdrawn from service.

17.

Left: Reflected in the still waters of the Birmingham-Worcester Canal near Dudley Port in March 1980, Class 81 No. 81014 heads towards Birmingham with an eastbound service. Air reservoirs have been substituted for the original second pantograph.

Geoff Dowling

18.

Above: No. 81018 leads Class 86/0 No. 86026 (now 86415 *Rotary International*) past Gretna Green on 5th June 1979 with a northbound train of chemical tanks. The Stone-Faiveley pantograph on the leading locomotive contrasts with the AEI cross-arm type on the Class 86.

Colin J. Marsden

19.

Below: On the night of 24th January 1981, No. 81016 languishes on one of the two Carlisle station centre roads awaiting an arrival from the south which it will take on to Glasgow. On 9th December 1982 near Linslade, this locomotive was severely damaged when it hit a piece of rail on the track that had fallen from another train, derailed and collided with an overbridge. It was found to be beyond economical repair and subsequently withdrawn from service.

20.
Although having been allocated to Glasgow Shields Road depot since January 1975, the Class 81 fleet make frequent visits to the South and are often utilised for empty coaching stock (ecs) workings between Euston station and Willesden carriage sidings (latterly Wembley InterCity Depot). All the class are now fitted with headlamps to replace the marker lights and are equipped for one-man operation. No. 81021 enters Euston on 15th June 1984 with ecs to form the 14.55 relief to Liverpool Lime Street (1F90).

21.
No. 81019 rests at the Euston buffer stops on 14th May 1984 having brought in the 00.28 Stirling-Euston "Royal Highlander" sleeping service.

22.
On the last day of January 1987, freshly painted No. 81010 moves ecs for Wembley away from Euston.

23.
Having just passed through Milton Keynes station, No. 81011 heads back to Derby on 30th May 1984 with an assortment of BR Technical Centre Research & Development vehicles in tow, consisting of RDB975136 'Laboratory 12', RDB977089, a former InterCity 125 Kitchen Car, RDB975427 'Laboratory 14' *Wren* and RDB977091, an experimental bus body on a Mk 1 underframe. Together the test train is used for investigating wheel to rail noise and vibration during running, which is measured by special on-board equipment.

Drawing C.
Type AL2 No. E3048 as originally constructed – 'A' side.

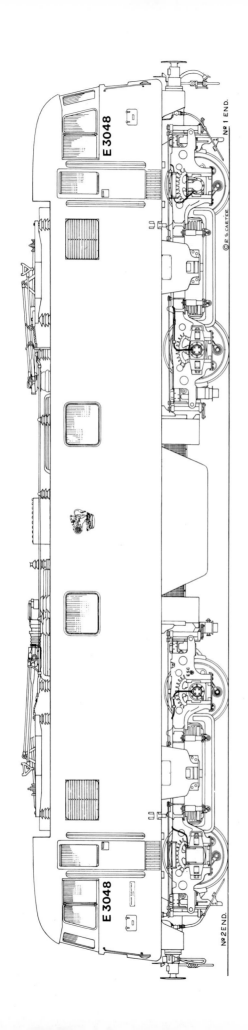

Drawing D.
Class 82 No. 82004 as modified in 1978 – 'B' side.

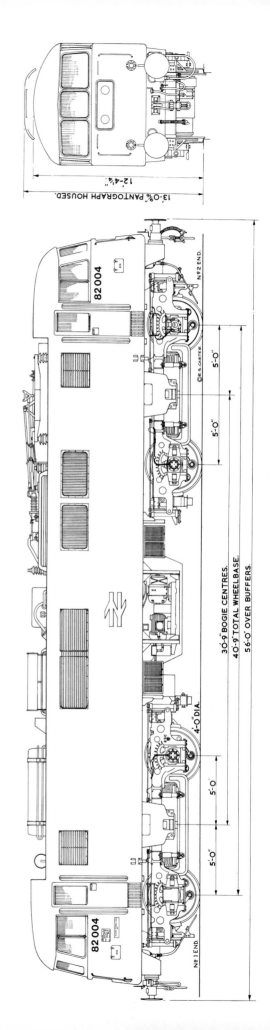

Class 82 (AL2)

Metropolitan-Vickers were the main contractors for the ten Class AL2s although, in reality, they were a part of AEI. It was no surprise, therefore, that a number of important components were of the same design as contained in the Class 81s, although the mechanical construction was entirely different, having been sub-contracted to Beyer Peacock of Gorton. Noted for their strong and powerful quality steam locomotives, it was entirely in keeping with the Beyer Peacock image and tradition that they should build upon a heavy load-bearing underframe with lightweight bodywork and the well-proven Commonwealth type of bogie. However, realising that the first of the type was coming out overweight to specification, lighter materials such as aluminium and fibreglass were substituted for some non-load bearing parts of the bodywork and selective electrical components were also removed and replaced with lighter versions. It was May 1960 before No. E3046 first appeared and nearly two years later before the order was complete.

Apart from the few years when all West Coast Main Line electric locomotives were on general AC lines allocation, the class was always allocated to Manchester Longsight until being put into store in 1982/83 after nearly 24 years service. Latterly, two remaining members of the small fleet were reinstated to traffic, allocated to Willesden depot and given a new lease of life on empty stock working to and from Euston, albeit restricted to a maximum speed of 40mph. Both have now been withdrawn however, and operationally, the type is extinct.

24.
The last of the AL2 fleet to be constructed was the only one of the first one hundred AC locomotives to have other than a Stone-Faiveley pantograph fitted, No. E3055 emerging from Gorton Works with an experimental AEI cross-arm type. This locomotive failed to survive long enough to receive a TOPS number as, following fire damage whilst hauling the 19.20 Manchester-Cardiff train in September 1966, it was finally cut up at Crewe Works in August 1970.

Colin J. Marsden collection

25.
Although the matt white cab roofs made the front end of the AC prototype locomotives reasonably visible from a distance, their main 'electric blue' shade of paintwork was not distinctive enough as a warning colour to track maintenance men, and the approach of a virtually silent machine at speeds of up to 100 mph was a very high-risk factor. Prior to the advent of the full-yellow end, a bright yellow panel was inserted below the cab window as seen here on No. E3052 (numbered 82006 until withdrawal in July 1983) departing from Euston station on 29th March 1967 with 1H42, the 16.00 to Manchester Piccadilly.

Rev. Graham Wise

27.
Above: Photographed from the higher reaches of Rail House at Crewe on 3rd March 1977, No. 82002 hauls the 06.30 Carlisle-Bescot freight.

Barry J. Nicolle

26.
Below left: Displaying the original 'B' side bodyside louvre arrangement and a freshly-applied new BR symbol on an unusual rectangular background, No. E3053 (82007 until withdrawal in July 1983) approaches Stafford station on 24th July 1979 with an afternoon express for Euston. One of the original two pantographs has been removed but the roof space has yet to be taken up with the main reservoirs.

John G. Glover

28.
Below: Prior to the obsolete route indicator panels being plated over and marker lights inserted, the roller blinds were set permanently with four noughts in the fashion shown in this illustration of No. 82005. It is approaching Carlisle on 3rd August 1978 with the 11.03 Birmingham New Street-Aberdeen train, which ran only on Tuesdays and Thursdays. From 17th March 1985, this locomotive was based at Willesden depot for working ecs to and from Euston and was finally withdrawn in September 1987.

31.
Passing Charnock Richard, between Preston and Wigan, on 24th August 1982 a lightweight semi-fast passenger service is taken south by No. 82008.

Gavin Morrison

29.
Above left: No. 82007 arrives at Euston on the evening of 21st October 1980 with a parcels train. At this time the eight survivors of the class were used principally for freight workings and had proved to be popular with both train crews and maintenance staff as they were the best riding of all the AC locomotive prototypes and, with their electrical circuits being by far the simplest, were also able to achieve the highest availability. This locomotive was withdrawn in July 1983.

Barry Edwards

30.
Left: The apparent clutter of the roof equipment on the AC electrics locomotives is shown to advantage in this view of No. 82004 at Birmingham New Street on 18th March 1978 hauling a parcels train for Manchester. Behind the three air reservoir tanks at the front can be observed the transformer radiator mounted horizontally at roof level, the conservator oil tank allowing the transformer lubricant to expand and contract, the AEI air-blast circuit breaker, the input connection and insulator to the main transformer, the rectifier cooling outlet ducting and the one remaining pantograph.

32.
Left: A study in steel. On 10th January 1981, No. 82001 departs from Manchester Piccadilly station with a Saturday inter-regional service. In the holding siding is a Cravens Class 104 diesel multiple unit and Class 86/0 No. 86009 which was later to become 86409. No. 82001 was withdrawn from service as life-expired on 19th July 1983 and eventually disposed of for scrap by Vic Berrys of Leicester in March 1985.

Colin J. Marsden

33.
Above: On 4th July 1981, No. 82008 stands adjacent to a Brush Class 47 diesel at Birmingham New Street station attached to the 09.18 Summer dated service from Penzance to Manchester Piccadilly.

Norman E. Preedy

34.
Below: At speed through Nuneaton station on Saturday, 27th March 1982, No. 82001 is utilised for a southbound 'Footex' special.

35.
Unsatisfactory ventilation resulted in revised bodyside louvres being fitted to the Class 82 fleet during the 1970s and the new arrangement is clearly shown with this illustration of No. 82006 passing Farrington Junction, south of Preston, on 10th August 1981 with a southbound semi-fast service.

Gavin Morrison

37.
Passing Castleton, north of Wolverton, on 27th October 1981, No. 82003 hauls a down air-braked service freight. This locomotive was withdrawn from service on 19th July 1983 and then stored at Crewe Works until moved to Willesden depot exactly one year later. There it was used to provide spares for the two temporarily reinstated locomotives of the class, Nos 82005 and 82008.

Michael J. Collins

36.
Below left: The lightweight 13.45 train from Liverpool Lime Street to Glasgow Central is pictured climbing to Shap Summit at Greenholme on 4th May 1981 powered by No. 82007.

John S. Whiteley

38.
Below: As the majority of the empty stock working in and out of Euston would involve InterCity liveried trains, it was decided that it would be a nice touch if a matching livery was applied to No. 82008 as seen here inside Willesden depot on 7th September 1987, together with Class 87/0s Nos 87004 *Britannia* and 87032 *Kenilworth*.

Drawing E.
Type AL3 No. E3033 as originally constructed – 'A' side.

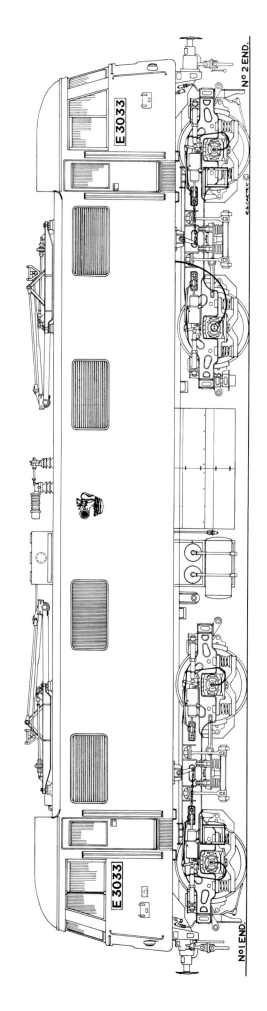

Drawing F.
Class 83 No. 83010 as modified – 'B' side.

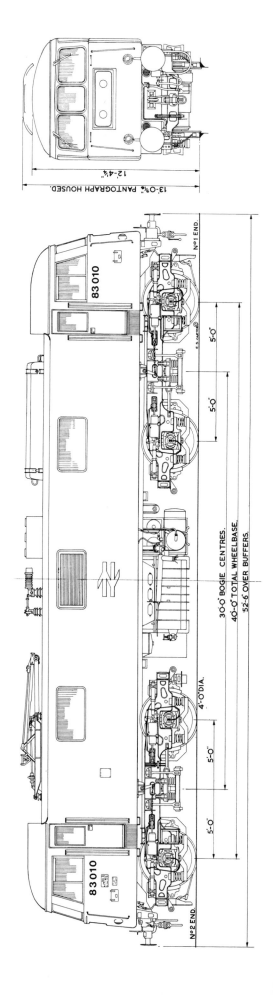

Class 83 (AL3)

The order for the 15-strong class AL3 AC electric locomotives was given to the English Electric Company and the building took place at their Vulcan Foundry works in Newton-le-Willows between July 1960 and July 1961 with one exception, the test-bed locomotive No. E3100, which was handed over in July 1962. Three of the fleet were to be constructed as freight locomotives with lower gear ratios but, in fact, only two appeared in this guise with the third one becoming E3100; both being converted to standard within a short period. The locomotives were light and the shortest of the prototypes with a length of 52ft 6in over the buffers, one foot shorter than the AL4, two and a half feet shorter than the AL2, three feet less than the AL1 and AL5 and a massive six feet shorter than the AL6. During the 1960s the fleet suffered a considerable problem with their mercury-arc rectifiers and a number of schemes to replace them with the silicon type as fitted to E3100 were discussed. Eventually BR decided to refurbish them at Doncaster Works on the same lines as that undertaken for the other prototypes with silicon rectifiers and dual braking and the work in this respect commenced in July 1970. As a result the locomotives performed satisfactorily but never quite to the standard of the BR constructed types and they were eventually withdrawn as surplus to requirements in 1983/84. Two members of the class however, were retained in operation and transferred to Willesden depot for use alongside the two Class 82s on empty stock workings to and from Euston.

39.
In pristine condition, No. E3025 (83002) arrives at Manchester Piccadilly on 8th September 1960 with a special working for the media from Crewe as a preview to the Manchester-Crewe electrification services. The BR 'lion and wheel' logo is positioned below the windows on this side of the body whereas, on the 'A' side, it was placed between the air-intake grilles high on the bodyside, as shown in picture 43.

Colin J. Marsden collection

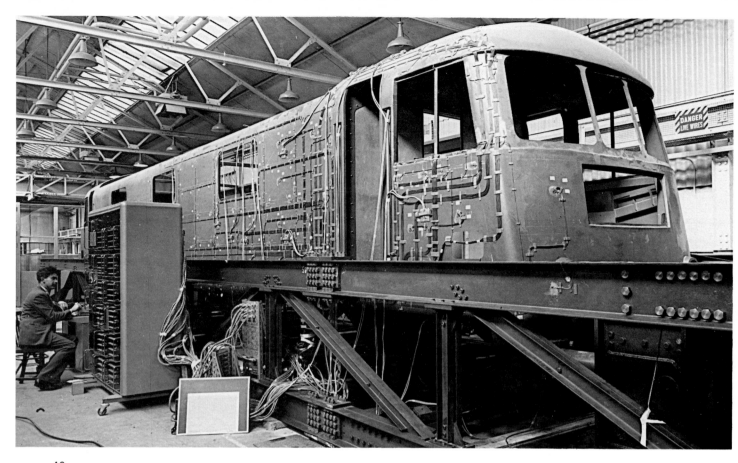

40.
A Type AL3 body shell was transported from Vulcan Foundry to the English Electric Mechanical Test Station at Whetstone in Leicestershire where tests were undertaken with it from June 1960 until February 1961. In this view the shell is in the compression test rig where it is wired up for static stress tests prior to having aerodynamic evaluation in the wind tunnel. On return to Vulcan Foundry, the shell was used in the construction of No. E3100.

Colin J. Marsden collection

41 & 42.
Left: Design of the English Electric Type AL3s was based upon both frame and body being fabricated as a stress-bearing unit using Cor-ten steel. The underframe was an integral part of the concept with the bodysides having girder frames and pillars of rectangular sections, as can be observed in this view taken inside Vulcan Foundry erecting shop in May 1960. *Above.* With the body framework now covered with both interior and exterior skins of steel sheeting, a production line of four AL3s is seen from atop the erecting shop crane in October 1960. Already fitted inside the nearer locomotive can be seen the main transformer which needs the full height of the body interior.

Both: Colin J. Marsden collection

43 & 44.

Before and after. The test-bed Class AL3/1 locomotive No. E3100 fitted with silicon rectifiers and transductors, being the first move towards thyristor control, ran extensive trials in the early 1960s, one of which is seen in the above view of the locomotive taken near Stafford in 1963. The test train includes a dynamometer car and three Class AL5 locomotives as a part of the load in order to provide additional rheostatic brake power for the adhesion trials. Although the unique No. E3100 had more than proved its worth it was nevertheless, a non-standard machine that required special drive training and, in consequence, its operational availability was restricted. It was therefore included in the complete fleet refurbishment undertaken at Doncaster Works and is seen, below, on display there on 1st October 1973 as standard Class 83 No. 83015 prior to commencing revenue earning service. The locomotive was eventually withdrawn from service in June 1983 but later reinstated and moved to Willesden depot to provide spares but, in fact, it was put to use on ecs workings where it was still deployed early in 1988.

Colin J. Marsden collection & M.A.E. Whatmough

45.
Heading a Euston-Liverpool Lime Street express passing Carpenders Park, Middlesex in June 1966, Class AL3 No. E3027 (83004) displays the half-yellow warning panel below the driver's cab that was utilised until the all-yellow front end became mandatory. The cab windows of the Type AL3s were set somewhat deeper in the front of the locomotives and, in consequence, a broader band of blue than shown on either the AL1s or AL2s separates them from the white of the fibreglass roof canopy. This locomotive sustained premature withdrawal in 1978 following the accident described in caption 267.

C.R. Lewis Coles

46.
With 'rail blue' livery and all-yellow ends now standard, No. 83012 emerges from Primrose Hill Tunnel north of Euston, on 6th June 1973 with an express for the Capital. It can be observed that the new BR symbol in metal alloy is now in use on the bodysides with white transfer numerals under the driving cab side window.

47.

Passing the once rival AEI premises at Rugby on 15th August 1975, English Electric Class 83 No. 83014 passes the station with a long parcels train that includes a Post Office TPO next to the locomotive.

Norman E. Preedy

48.

On the evening of 28th September 1984, No. 83012 waits to depart from Euston for Willesden carriage sidings with empty stock of the "Clansman" express. This train had left Inverness that morning at 10.30 and arrived at its destination on time at 21.11 following scheduled stops at Aviemore, Perth, Stirling, Carlisle, Preston, Crewe, Wolverhampton, Birmingham New Street, Birmingham International, Coventry and, lastly, Watford Junction.

Brian Beer

49.
In the entirely different setting of Dillicar, near Tebay, No. 83012 is photographed under a very stormy sky on 4th May 1981 passing over the site of the old water troughs and hauling the 15.02 service from Glasgow Central to Liverpool Lime Street.

John S. Whiteley

50.
On 30th August 1979, Class 83 No. 83006 leads Class 85 No. 85004 away from Carlisle Kingmoor yard with a haul of tanks and passes Class 25/2 Bo-Bo diesel locomotive No. 25211. Of the three locomotives, only the Class 85 has not been withdrawn and is still in traffic.

Gavin Morrison

51.
For inter-regional services running to the South on the West Coast Main Line, the 25kV AC overhead electrification ends at Mitre Bridge Junction where it is necessary to change over to diesel traction. On 8th March 1979, Class 83 No. 83010 has brought in an empty stock train from Manchester bound for Clapham Junction and is about to be replaced for the remaining short part of the journey by BRC&W Class 33/0 Bo-Bo diesel No. 33009. The electric locomotive was withdrawn from service in July 1983.

Colin J. Marsden

52.
For several years after completion of the West Coast electrification, the Freightliner services between Willesden and Scotland, North Wales and the North of England were entrusted to the Class 81-85 fleet, as depicted in this view of No. 83001 passing the site of the old Bushey water troughs en route to Willesden Freightliner Terminal (FLT) on the misty morning of 29th April 1978. Today these services have been rationalised and much heavier loads are carried, usually by double-heading Class 86 or 87 locomotives.

53.
On 22nd September 1979, No. 83008 heads south from Crewe with a relief express for Euston. This view compares with the illustration of No. 83001 opposite and clearly shows the original placement of the three bodyside windows on the 'B' side, with the centre one now replaced by a grille. The 'A' side retains the original four grilles.

M.A.E. Whatmough

54.
Painted in attractive InterCity livery of light and dark grey with red band, No. 83012 had an extended lease of life in use for ecs workings in and out of Euston where it is seen on 1st May 1987 hauling the stock of an earlier arrival from Northampton, back to what is now known as the Wembley InterCity Depot.

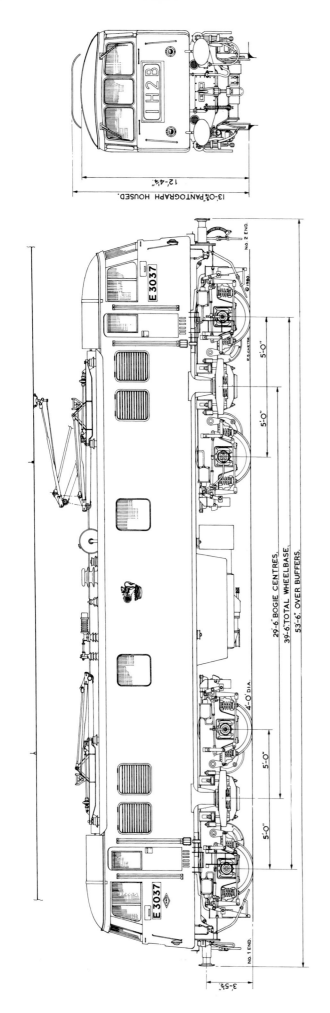

Drawing G.
Type AL4 No. E3037 as originally constructed – 'A' side.

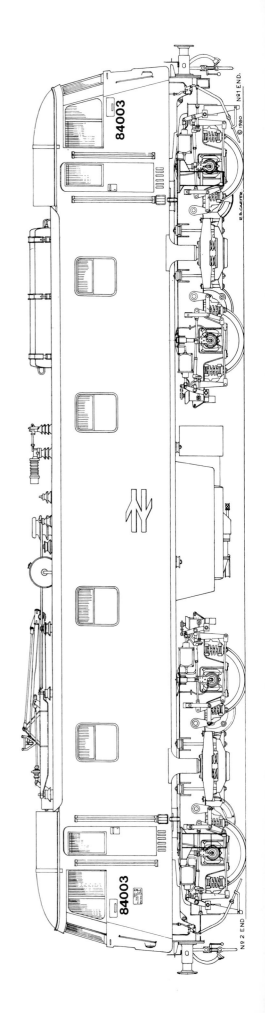

Drawing H.
Class 84 No. 84003 as modified – 'B' side.

Class 84 (AL4)

The General Electric Company (GEC) sub-contracted to the North British Locomotive Company of Glasgow, both design and construction of the ten locomotives which made up this class. The locomotive bodies were designed to be integral with the underframe and the structure used a preponderance of mild steel with body structure clad in welded sheet steel giving a very sleek external finish. The first of the class, No. E3036 emerged from Hyde Park Works, Springburn in May 1960 and the last of the small fleet appeared in March 1961. By 1962 one of the class had been returned to GEC for investigation as they were found to be rough riding in the extreme and were having the same problem with rectifier failure as encountered with the type AL3s. Various modifications were made but problems persisted and in 1967 nine of the fleet were put into long term storage alongside the class AL3s at the closed Bury steam shed with No. E3043 being sent to Rugby Testing Station. Whilst in store, one or two of the disgraced locomotives were brought out and exhibited at depot 'open days', such as Tyseley, Bristol Bath Road, Crewe and Kingmoor, as an example of modern electric traction! Completion of the West Coast Main Line electrification from Crewe to Glasgow brought about the resurrection of both type AL3s and AL4s however, as it was cheaper to refurbish these locomotives to work the extension and build only 36 new Class 87s, rather than build some 50 new machines to meet the requirement. Unfortunately the work undertaken at Doncaster Works did not overcome a number of the built-in problems affecting the fleet which still suffered an unacceptably high failure rate and withdrawals commenced in 1977. By 1980 none were left in traffic but No. 84001 is preserved as an example of early AC electric locomotion at the National Railway Museum, York, and former No. 84009 is now a mobile load bank for testing overhead electrical equipment for the Research Department.

55.
The last class AL4 locomotive to be constructed, No. E3045 (later 84010), is photographed out of use at Longsight depot in 1962. Showing the 'A' side of the body that contains four grilles and two fixed windows with BR 'lion and wheel' between them, one of the windows, in fact, being missing.

Norman E. Preedy

56.
Passing the radio telescope at Jodrell Bank, near Goostrey, on the Crewe-Manchester line on 14th July 1960, the second locomotive of type AL4, No. E3037 (84002), hauls a test train consisting of ex-LMS stock.

Colin J. Marsden collection

57.
Hauling a test train of loaded ballast wagons with a brakevan at both ends, the first of the type AL4s, No. E3036 (84001), passes East Didsbury shortly after construction. Some detail differences from other prototype AC electric locomotive classes included the unique oval-shaped buffers and the rather untidy bufferbeam arrangement. The electric tail lights are also placed slightly higher than on the other types and the original route indicator panel sported a polished metal surround.

Colin J. Marsden collection

58.
Crewe North Junction in the early 1960s. No. E3044 (84009) leaves Crewe station and heads for the Manchester line with an express from Cardiff with an unidentified Stanier 'Black 5' 4-6-0 steam locomotive running alongside with a semi-fast service.

Colin J. Marsden collection

59.
Now in corporate 'rail blue' livery with full yellow ends and new-style BR logo on the bodyside, refurbished No. 84001 hurries towards Wembley Central on 26th June 1973 entrusted with the 16.45 Euston-Glasgow "Executive" express.

60.
Towards the end of their working life, the class 84's occasional passenger train outings relied mainly upon their rarity value on enthusiasts' specials. On Easter Saturday 1980, Gresley Class A3 Pacific No. 4472 *Flying Scotsman* prepares to leave Carlisle with the southbound "Cumbrian Mountain Express" which it has taken over from No. 84002 which runs alongside prior to returning south 'light engine'.

John Whitehouse

61.
On 16th September 1978, the "AC/DC Railtour" provided for Class 84 haulage and the special working is seen here en route from Birmingham to Manchester at Bescot behind No. 84002. This locomotive was withdrawn from stock in September 1980 and sold to GEC for use as a generator, being finally sent by road to a Stockport scrap dealer in December 1982.

John Whitehouse

62.
Specially prepared for the occasion, No. 84001 passes Bushey on 29th April 1978 with the outward "North West Rambler Railtour" organised jointly by two concerns who ran many railtours at this time, DAA Railtours and the Diesel & Electric Group. This view clearly shows the four drop-light windows contained in the body of the 'B' side of the locomotive, one being partly open.

63.
Hauling the "Knotty Rambler" special from Congleton to Brighton on the same day, No. 84002 hares through Bushey. It will haul the train as far as Mitre Bridge Junction in West London where a diesel locomotive will take over.

64.

On 7th June 1980, No. 84010 arrives at Crewe station with a short van train that was typical of the type of duty that the Class 84s undertook during their final days. This particular locomotive was withdrawn five months after this photograph was taken and with No. 84002 was sold to GEC at Trafford Park, Manchester for use as a generator. It met the same fate as its sister locomotive, described in caption 61.

Norman E. Preedy

65.

Destined to be withdrawn from service just 25 days after this view was taken, No. 84003 leaves Birmingham International station on 18th October 1980 with a return Motor Show excursion special for Manchester. After withdrawal, the locomotive was taken into Departmental stock in order to supply spares for No. ADB968021 shown opposite.

John Chalcraft

66.
Former No. 84009, now carrying the Research Department Service No. ADB968021, is seen inside Ilford 'B' Shop on 29th April 1986 in use as a load bank in connection with the conversion of TSOT stock to InterCity Buffet RMBTs. The livery which the majority of R&D stock receives is red and blue with the red uppermost and full-yellow ends extending to the cab side windows. The round non-standard headlight is a recent acquisition.

67.
Withdrawn from stock on 26th October 1979, No. 84008 still awaits its fate on the scrap line outside the Crewe Melt Shop on 9th April 1987.

Drawing I
Type AL5 No. E3058 as originally constructed – 'A' side.

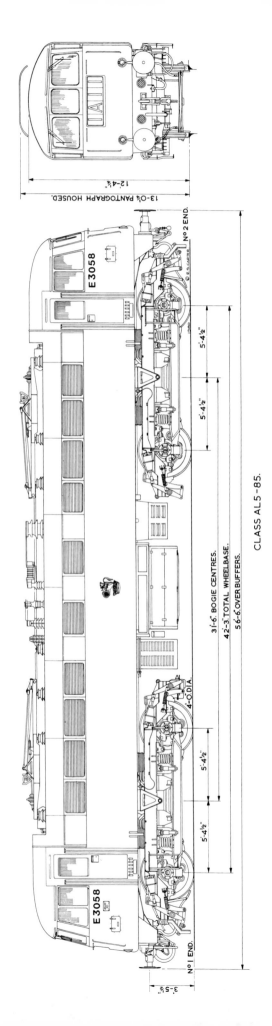

13'-0⅛" PANTOGRAPH HOUSED.

12'-4½"

E3058

E3058

No 1 END.

No 2 END.

© E.S.CARTER.

3'-5¾"

5'-4½"

5'-4½"

5'-4½"

5'-4½"

4'-0 DIA.

31'-6" BOGIE CENTRES.

42'-3" TOTAL WHEELBASE.

56'-6" OVER BUFFERS.

CLASS AL5 - 85.

Drawing J.
Class 85 No. 85020 as modified – 'B' side.

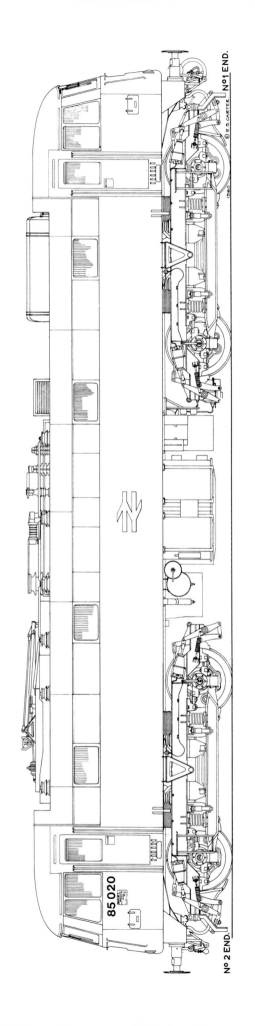

85 020

No 2 END.

No 1 END.

© E.S.CARTER.

Class 85 (AL5)

Of the 100 prototype AC electric locomotives ordered by British Transport Commission, 60 were constructed by four outside industry manufacturers and 40 to a design produced by the Eastern Region CM&EE at BR's Doncaster Works. These latter machines become known as Type AL5 and later Class 85. Eastern Region become involved as, initially, both East and West Coast main lines were to be electrified simultaneously. Basically the fleet are similar to the Class 81 design with AEI equipment being used but they differ in two particular aspects with the use of semi-conductor rectifiers and rheostatic braking which, after initial problems, is now fully automatic. The semi-integral body construction involved the underframe being welded to the lower half of the bodysides to form a deep trough, with the upper half of the body of a lightweight construction that was made easily removable for works visits. The between-cab layout was similar to the other four prototype classes with the electrical equipment situated on one side and a walkway from cab to cab on the other. In the same way as the Types AL1 – 4, all were initially fitted with a pantograph at each end of the roof but, along with the other types, the No. 1 fitting was removed and replaced by air reservoir tanks when the 1970's refurbishments took place. Of the original 40 locomotives, 35 remain in traffic at the time of writing, used principally for freight and slower passenger duties as, although sturdy performers, their moderate riding qualities are not conducive to the sustained high-speed running requirement of present day InterCity services.

68.
Other than the addition of the front yellow warning panel, Type AL5 No. E3074 (later 85019) is in original condition in this view taken at Watford Junction in 1966. The unfitted southbound freight in tow is a real period piece and looks particularly incongruous being hauled by, what was at this time, a modern electric locomotive. The line of bodyside grilles as seen here on the 'A' side of the locomotive, which contains the electrical equipment, contrasts with the cab to cab walkway side 'B', as seen overleaf, which is fitted with four glazed windows.

C.R. Lewis Coles

69.
Above: Newly constructed Class AL5 locomotives Nos E3063 and E3065 (now 85008 and 85009) are posed for the camera inside Allerton depot in December 1961 alongside a Type AL2. All the Class 85 fleet have been allocated to Crewe Electric Depot since 1973/74.

Colin J. Marsden collection

70.
Below: Attached to all-maroon Mk 1 stock, No. E3092 (later 85037) waits to leave Liverpool Lime Street station on 25th June 1964 with the Euston bound "Manxman" express, named thus as it connected at Liverpool with the Isle of Man ferries.

C.R. Lewis Coles

71.
Displayed to the public in Manchester Central station goods yard as part of the 'Modern Look' exhibition on 19th March 1962, Type AL5 No. E3058 (85003) is accompanied by 'Peak' class diesel No. D62 (to become No. 45143 *5th Royal Inniskilling Dragoon Guards 1685-1985*) and 'Coronation' Class Pacific steam locomotive No. 46256 *Sir William A. Stanier, F.R.S.*, a name perpetuated on Class 86/1 AC electric No. 86101.

A.W. Martin

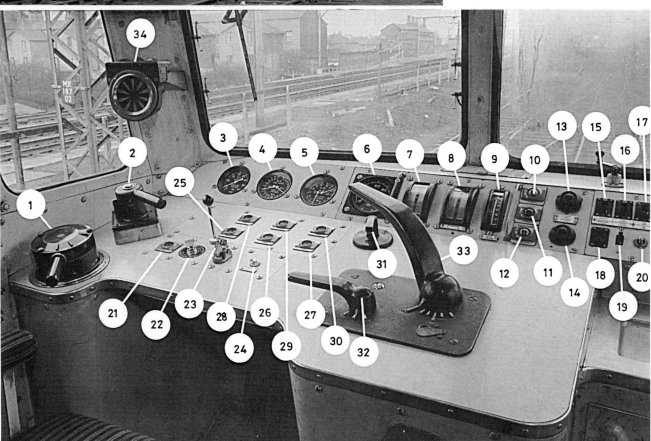

72.
In an attempt to avoid the consequences regarding lack of standardisation that were disastrously encountered with their pilot scheme diesel locomotives, the British Transport Commission laid down strict guidelines for the various manufacturers to follow in constructing the prototype AC electric locomotives. Principal among these was a required uniformity for the method of driving, coupled with the lay-out of the cab controls as illustrated here on a Class 85.

Colin J. Marsden collection

1. Train brake valve
2. Straight air-brake valve
3. Main reservoir gauge
4. Brake cylinder gauge
5. Vacuum train pipe/chamber gauge
6. Speedometer
7. Traction Motors 1 & 2 current indicator
8. Traction Motors 3 & 4 current indicator
9. Notch indicator
10. Line indicator
11. Fault indicator
12. Train heat on indicator
13. Indicator lights dimmer control
14. Instrument lights dimmer control
15. Demister switch
16. Footrest warmer switch
17. Cab heat switch
18. Instrument light switch
19. Route indicator light switch
20. Tail light switch
21. Anti-slip brake button
22. Windscreen wiper valve
23. Horn control valve
24. AWS reset button
25. Exhauster stop button
26. Pantograph down button
27. Train heat on button
28. Exhauster start button
29. Pantograph up/reset button
30. Train heat off button
31. Power brake change-over
32. Master switch
33. Power handle
34. AWS indicator

73.

Left: Providing the motive power for a lorry transporter train, Class 85 No. E3082 (still to be re-numbered 85027) and Class 83 No. 83013 pass southwards through Oxenholme station on 11th June 1974 during the time that the BR TOPS re-numbering scheme was being implemented. The Class 85 pictured here suffered severe fire damage at King's Langley on 23rd April 1983 and was, subsequently, withdrawn from service, being cut-up at Crewe Works in March 1985.

74.

Below left: On 6th June 1973, No. E3078 (85023) approaches the summit of Camden Bank from Primrose Hill Tunnel heading towards Euston with an InterCity express.

75.

Below: An unpleasant Merseyside drizzle is temporarily relieved by a flash of watery sunshine on 23rd September 1976 as Class 85 No. 85038 (right) and Class 86/2 No. 86216 (later to be named *Meteor*) await departure from Liverpool Lime Street station with, respectively, the 10.04 to Euston and a van train for Birmingham.

76.
Above: Attached to six 12tonne type VWV box vans in the station siding at Rugby on 21st April 1979, No. 85013 awaits the scheduled time to have the pantograph switched into place and to move away northwards.

77.
Below: The customary coaching stock for railway enthusiast or football supporter specials is elderly Mk1s, as attached to No. 85003 hauling a northbound 'Footex' north of Carpenders Park in Middlesex on 29th April 1978. With both factions containing a minority of the mindless, BR's reasoning is probably sound, although they will only admit to the cause being due to weekend stock shortages!

78.
Right top: On the chill but brilliantly clear morning of 9th February 1983, No. 85038 heads south at Grayrigg in Cumbria with the 08.23 Glasgow Central/08.06 Edinburgh-Nottingham InterCity service, the two trains having merged at Carstairs.

79.
Right, bottom: In ex-works condition and in a Christmas card setting near Berkhamsted, No. 85008 climbs the Chiltern hills with a northbound 'Freightliner' service on 9th December 1981 and heads towards the summit at Tring.
Rev. Graham Wise

80.
The twelve 'cartics' attached to No. 85010 contain a valuable haul of some 74 Ford Cortinas and Fiestas from the Ford plant at Dagenham. They travel north near Shap on 4th June 1979 heading for Garston on Merseyside.

Colin J. Marsden

81.
On 26th November 1987, a very mixed air-braked service freight from Willesden travels away from the London suburbs through Kenton hauled by No. 85040. The preponderance of ferry wagons that make up the train, identify it as emanating from Dover as the 03.55 'Speedlink' to Willesden Brent sidings.

82.
Approaching Rugby on 21st April 1979, No. 85009 powers an up parcels train and passes a Class 08 shunter No. 08684 acting as station pilot.

83.
With their two disparate body-sides on view to the cameraman, Nos 85007 and 85027 pass alongside the Grand Union Canal at Northchurch, on the climb to Tring Summit, 15th January 1981, hauling the 13.12 Freightliner from Tilbury to Manchester, Trafford Park.

Rev. Graham Wise

84.
On 22nd February 1986, No. 85020 speeds northward near Oxenholme with a rake of mixed-liveried coaching stock forming the 07.26 Coventry-Glasgow Central cross-country InterCity service.

John Broughton

85.
Contrasting front ends at Manchester Piccadilly on a wet 1st June 1984. Class 31/4 A1A-A1A diesel No. 31434 leaves the station with the 18.00 vans train for Derby whilst Class 85 Bo-Bo electric locomotive No. 85002 awaits departure with the 18.15 passenger service for London, Euston.

86.
Mailbags have been loaded into the two vans that make up a northbound parcels train at Rugby station on the late evening of 2nd March 1984 and No. 85006 at the head will shortly move out into the night.

87.
Another night service, but this one for passengers, is seen at Carlisle on 24th January 1981 with No. 85032 powering the 17.03 train from Glasgow Central to Manchester Victoria.

Drawing K.
Type AL6 No. E3180 as originally constructed – 'B' side.

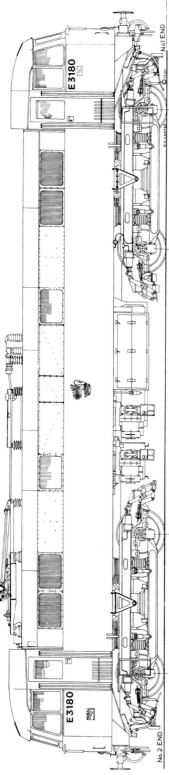

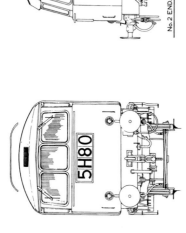

Drawing L.
Class 86/0 No. 86026 - 'A' side.

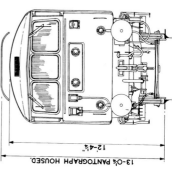

13-0½ PANTOGRAPH HOUSED.
12-4½"

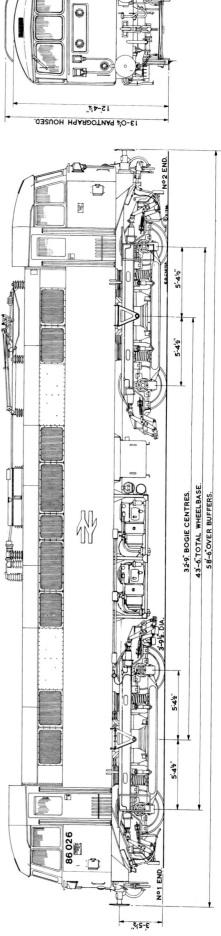

No2 END.
B.S.CENTRE.
5'-4½"
5'-4½"
No1 END.
B.S.CENTRE.
5'-4½"
5'-4½"
3-9½" DIA.
3-5⅜"
32'-9" BOGIE CENTRES.
43'-6" TOTAL WHEELBASE.
58'-6" OVER BUFFERS.

86026

Class 86/0 (AL6)

After experience with their fleet of 100 prototype AC locomotives of Types AL1-AL5, British Rail ordered the same number of second-generation locomotives which were classified AL6 and later 86, the sub-classifications 86/0 to 86/5 coming about later. Building was divided between English Electric at Vulcan Foundry and BR at the Doncaster Plant with a 60 to 40 split in favour of the former; electrical equipment being supplied jointly by English Electric and AEI. Body superstructure, bogies and suspensions were similar to the AL5s but the new types, helped by being two feet longer overall and with smaller wheels allowing more headroom, had a much-improved internal layout.

The first of the new fleet emanated from Vulcan Foundry in July 1965 with the first from Doncaster arriving two months later. Only one pantograph was fitted and, contrary to previous practice for AC locomotives, the traction motors were axle-hung, on the lines of successful diesel-electric types. This arrangement transpired not to be suited however, and the whole class was eventually re-equipped with new wheels and suspension, as more fully described under Classes 86/1 and 86/2. Despite construction allowing for the cab walkway to be in the centre of the body, the two body-sides of the fleet nevertheless differed, with side 'A' having a bank of nine air louvre grilles and side 'B' two windows plus two grilles. The most noticeable external difference from the first generation fleet however, was in the shape of the cab front where the section below the cab windows was flat with only the top half sloping backwards in the previous way. Like the Type AL5, the upper half of the body was designed for complete removal between the cabs, thus facilitating easier access during works visits. None of the fleet now survive in original condition, the last changeover of wheels and suspensions occurring during 1987 when No. 86007 became No. 86407.

88.
Class AL6 No. E3112 (later 86006/86406) hauls a train of Ford products through Watford Junction in October 1965 and displays the interim colour scheme given to the fleet of 'rail blue' with light beige cab roof panels, off-white cab window surrounds and red buffer beams. Cast alloy numerals are still in use together with the BR 'lion and wheel' crest.

C.R. Lewis Coles

89.
The use of a massive rotary jig enables this type AL6 body, under construction in Vulcan Works, Newton-le-Willows, early in 1966, to be turned to any position for welding.

Colin J. Marsden collection

90.
In March 1966, No. E3190 (later 86210 *City of Edinburgh*) arrives at Willesden yard with a parcels train. This view clearly shows the window side of the body and also the grille in the cab roof covering the space containing the twin air-horns, these being positioned behind the buffer beam on the earlier types.

Colin T. Gifford

91.
With a rake of four Pullman coaches bringing up the rear of the train, the down "Liverpool Pullman" passes near to the site where Milton Keynes station was later constructed. The locomotive providing traction is No. E3163 which was to become, respectively, 86018, 86318 and finally, 86418.

Colin J. Marsden collection

92.
Consisting of all-Pullman stock, the 07.50 Manchester Piccadilly-Euston service, the "Manchester Pullman", rolls down Camden Bank into Euston station headed by No. E3139 (later 86043/86257 *Snowdon*).

Colin J. Marsden collection

93.
Acting as a relief service to the ''Manchester Pullman'' which had departed ten minutes earlier, the second train of the day from London to Manchester, the 08.05 from Euston, tops Camden Bank on 6th June 1973 powered by No. E3167 (now 86228 *Vulcan Heritage)*. As can be observed, the locomotive has received standard overall-yellow front ends with current BR cast-alloy symbol but retains a pre-TOPS number.

94.
Today, empty coaching stock workings to and from Euston are not quite so prevalent as they were in the 1970s as many trains are cleaned and reversed in the station. On 16th May 1973, two trains of ecs are halted by adverse signals on the Camden Bank relief lines and await clearance before proceeding to the washing plant. The locomotives are Nos E3178 and E3140 which, today, are Nos 86244 *The Royal British Legion* and 86501 *Talyllyn*, respectively, the latter being one of ten Class 86/2s reclassified to 86/5 in May 1988 following regearing for dedicated work with the Freightliner Sector.

95.
The code 1A25 displayed in the route indicator panel indicates that this train is the up "Emerald Isle Express', a fairly short-lived service between Liverpool Lime Street and Euston. On 6th June 1973, the train locomotive bursting from Primrose Hill Tunnel, is No. E3106 (now 86214 *Sans Pareil).*

96.
Soon after sunrise on 29th September 1972, the 21.45 sleeping car service from Glasgow Central passes Primrose Hill on the last lap of the journey to Euston hauled by No. E3168 (now 86230 *The Duke of Wellington).*

98.
Shortly after a scheduled 04.50 arrival at Euston on 14th December 1975, the 00.25 'small hours of the night' service from Manchester Piccadilly is allowed to stay in platform 7 for a short while with the majority of the passengers, understandably, still asleep. Bearing the train reporting number of 1A01 is No. 86033 (now 86433 *Wulfruna*).

97.
Left: In blizzard conditions on Christmas Eve 1970, a Manchester Piccadilly-Euston express enters Stockport station behind No. E3133 (now 86236 *Josiah Wedgwood*).

Brian Beer

99.
Below: Racing upgrade through the Lune Gorge, near Tebay, on 12th June 1974, No. 86004 (now 86404) effortlessly powers the twelve Mk 2 'air-cons' that make up the 11.45 Euston-Glasgow Central express.

100.
Pullmans on the up slow line! At Carpender's Park No. 86013 (now 86413 *County of Lancashire*) heads a Manchester United football special on FA Cup Final Day 1979, bound for Wembley Central and consisting of the "Manchester Pullman" coaching stock. The route indicator blinds were no longer in use at this stage and until such time as their panels could be altered to contain new marker lights, they were set to show four noughts.

Antony Guppy

101.
Hauling a southbound Freightliner past Basford Hall, Crewe, on 4th April 1979, No. 86020 (86420) also displays 0000.

Gavin Morrison

102.
With a haul of southbound steel coil, Nos 86038 and 86024 (now 86438 and 86424) cruise downgrade at Greenholme, near Shap, on 9th February 1983. As can be observed by the jumper cable and receptacle added to the front end adjacent to the new sealed beam headlights, these locomotives are fitted for multiple-unit working.

103.
The 09.15 from Glasgow Central and the 09.23 from Edinburgh join up at Carstairs and continue as one train to Birmingham New Street. On the very frosty morning of 26th January 1980, the scene is Wreay, south of Carlisle, as No 86004 (now 86404) speeds south with the train.

104.
With no sign of traditional Manchester weather, No. 86032 (86432 *Brookside*) fairly sparkles in the summer sunshine of 20th August 1980, as it snakes into Piccadilly station with empty InterCity coaching stock for a departure later in the day.

Gavin Morrison

105
On 1st March 1984, No. 86030 (86430 *Scottish National Orchestra*) departs southwards from Nuneaton with Speedlink coal hoppers brought in from Toton yard by Class 45/0 'Peak' diesel No. 45077. The train reversed here.

Class 86/1

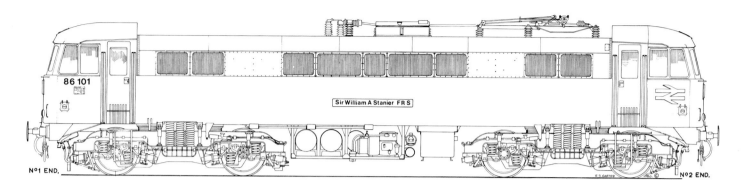

Drawing M.
Class 86/1 No. 86101 in the condition that it was to be seen in 1978 after naming. The modifications shown took place in 1972.

106.
As a result of the decision to extend electrification of the West Coast Main Line to Glasgow Central, a further 34 locomotives, later increased to 36, were authorised to be constructed, and became Class 87. To gain service experience of much of the new equipment that was to be incorporated into the new machines, three of the Vulcan Foundry built Class 86 were modified at Crewe Works in 1972 with new BP9 bogies, having frame-mounted traction motors and 'Flexicoil' suspension. Nos E3143, E3150 and E3191 were given classification 86/1 and eventually all three were named after famous locomotive engineers. After receiving the modifications, but prior to receiving the new number 86103, No. 86203 is pictured at Preston with a southbound special test train. Observe the offset quartz headlight which was fitted to two of the three Class 86/1 locomotives.
Colin J. Marsden collection

107.
With the British Thomson-Houston Works buildings of GEC forming the background to this photograph at Rugby on 16th June 1979, No. 86101 heads an express for Euston and displays the nameplates of *Sir William A Stanier FRS* which were unveiled at Liverpool Lime Street station in October 1978.

Gavin Morrison

108.
On the evening of 2nd March 1984, the usual electric multiple unit to form the 17.30 semi-fast service to Euston was not available and the unusual replacement was No. 86102 *Robert A. Riddles* and five Mk 1 coaches as recorded here during the mandatory Rugby stop. This locomotive does not display the headlight fitted to the other two members of the type.

109.
Sporting InterCity Sector livery, No. 86103 *André Chapelon* passes Milton Keynes at speed on 30th January 1988 with the 09.50 Blackpool North-Euston train. In line with the Class 87 and some of Classes 86/2 and 86/4, the three locomotives of Class 86/1 are now fitted with a Brecknell Willis 'Highspeed' pantograph which assists in enabling the locomotive's maximum speed to be increased from 100 to 110 mph.

Drawing N.
Class 86/2 No. 86209 as modified in 1972 showing the 'B' side.

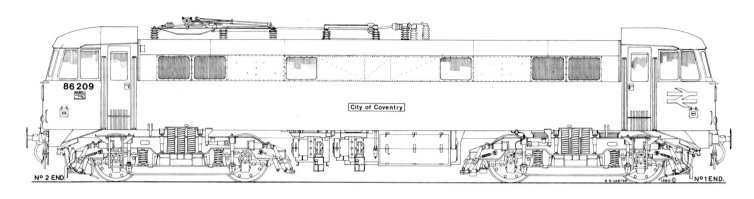

86 209

City of Coventry

Nº 2 END.

R.S.CARTER   1980 ©   Nº 1 END.

Drawing O.
The SAB resilient wheel as fitted to all Class 86/2, 86/3, 86/4 and 86/5.

1. TYRE INTEGRAL WITH CENTRE DISC.
2. OUTER DISC.
3. WHEELHUB INTEGRAL WITH INNER DISC.
4. PAIRS OF RUBBER PADS COMPRESSED
   BETWEEN OUTER, CENTRE, AND INNER DISCS.
5. SECURING BOLT OUTER DISC TO WHEELHUB.
6. DISTANCE BOLT OUTER DISC TO INNER DISC.

'A'

'A'

1
2
4
5
3
6

Class 86/2

Although the Class 86 fleet proved more reliable in service and easier to maintain than the first-generation AC electric locomotives of Classes 81 to 85, problems were encountered with bogie frame fractures and track damage. This resulted from the heavier unsprung weight of the axle-hung traction motors, a situation that posed quite serious problems as electrification through to Scotland would result in very heavy utilisation of the class at high speeds. An interim, partial solution was found in the use of SAB resilient wheels as designed and made by Svenska Aktiebolaget Bromsregulator of Malmo, Sweden, where only the weight of the tyres and tyre disc actually rest unsprung on the rails. The axle, axle-boxes, springs and motors are protected by the resilience brought about with the internal rubber-cushioning. Earlier experiments with locomotive No. E3173 using 'Flexicoil' suspension were very successful and it was therefore decided to rebuild 58 of the Class 86 fleet with this suspension and the resilient wheels. At the same time they would be refurbished for top link duties with the latest rolling stock. The completed locomotives were classified 86/2 with those in original condition becoming known as 86/0 and having a top speed limit of 80mph imposed.

110.
After modifications to bogies and suspensions were completed, the locomotives affected were re-numbered into the TOPS category of 86/2. No. 86228 (formerly E3167) storms Shap on 12th June 1974 with the 09.00 InterCity express from Euston to Carlisle. All the Class 86/2 have since been named with this one now bearing the legend *Vulcan Heritage,* in recognition of the part played by the English Electric Vulcan Foundry in BR locomotive design and construction.

111.
Bound for Scotland, InterCity 1S71 is seen at speed near Oxenholme on 11th June 1974 in charge of No. 86210. Originally allocated the name *Hardwicke,* this locomotive was then to be called *City of Preston* until it was realised that Preston was not, in fact, a city! The name eventually decided upon was the one still carried today, *City of Edinburgh,* and which was received at Edinburgh station on 27th February 1979.

112.
Restarting the 10.00 Liverpool Lime Street-Euston InterCity service from the scheduled Coventry stop on 5th January 1975, No. 86230 carries an incorrect train reporting number of 1A04 as this train was, in fact, 1A14. The locomotive now carries the name *The Duke of Wellington.*

113.
Emerging into Liverpool Lime Street station from the gloom of the arches beyond Russell Street Tunnel on 23rd September 1976, the 08.14 Rugby-Liverpool Lime Street service is powered by No. 86261 which today carries the name *Driver John Axon G.C.* The standard Stone-Faiveley pantograph initially fitted to all but ten of the original fleet is clearly shown in this illustration.

114.
The last ten AL6 locomotives constructed were fitted with an AEI cross-arm pantograph instead of the Stone-Faiveley type shown above. In practice, however, the type of pantograph fitted to a particular locomotive at any one time can be of either type as a result of replacement following accident damage or wear and tear. The AEI cross-arm variety is fitted here to No. 86213 (since named *Lancashire Witch*) heading the 10.40 Wolverhampton-Euston express through Marston Green, near Birmingham, on 6th October 1979.

115.
Passing Basford Hall, south of Crewe, on 4th June 1979, No. 86221 powers the "Manchester Pullman" southwards for Euston. Previously named *Vesta*, this locomotive now carries the plates *BBC Look East.*

Gavin Morrison

116.
On 22nd September 1976, the 16.12 Manchester Piccadilly-Euston InterCity service draws to a halt at the scheduled Stockport stop behind No. 86237, since named *Sir Charles Hallé.* In the opposite platform is the tail end of the 13.55 Euston-Manchester Piccadilly train hauled by an out-of-sight Class 86/0 No. 86013 (now 86403).

117.
The 12.45 express for Glasgow Central accelerates away from Euston station on 16th September 1978 powered by No. 86249, which was named *County of Merseyside* at Liverpool Lime Street station on 7th September 1981.

118.
Flashing through the Hertfordshire countryside between Bushey and Carpenders Park, the 06.10 Carlisle-Euston service was some ten minutes early when photographed on 30th June 1976. Providing power is No. 86244 which now carries the name *The Royal British Legion*.

119.

Carlisle station on 3rd November 1979. On the left, a since withdrawn Swindon built Class 126 diesel multiple unit, set No. 407 is led by motor brake second class car No. SC51037 and forms the 14.00 service to Ayr. Standing at the opposite platform, No. 86247 (now named *Abraham Darby)* has charge of the 08.10 InterCity service from Birmingham New Street to Glasgow Central and on the right, Class 87 No. 87029 *Earl Marischal* pauses for a refreshment stop with a Bristol Temple Meads-Edinburgh ADEX on which no buffet or trolley services had been provided. Observe that the original route indicator panel on the dmu has been plated over and marker lights, fitted whereas the one on the Class 86/2 has sealed beam headlamps.

Graham Scott-Lowe

120.

Forming a southbound express on 9th September 1978, Mk 3 coaching stock is hurried towards Stowe Hill Tunnel, between Rugby and Roade, and is powered by No. 86223. Originally carrying the plates *Hector,* this locomotive was later renamed *Norwich Union.*

Gavin Morrison

121.
Taking the fast road through Rugby on 21st April 1979, No. 86214 (since named *Sans Pareil)* has charge of the 11.00 InterCity express from Manchester Piccadilly to Euston and sports an AEI cross-arm pantograph.

122.
Also with an AEI pantograph, No. 86231 passes Lichfield Trent Valley at speed on 1st March 1984 heading the 15.00 InterCity working from Euston to Liverpool Lime Street. The plates *Lady of the Lake* were allocated to this locomotive, but these were never fitted as it was named *Starlight Express* at Euston station on 1st October 1984 by members of the cast of the prestigious musical show of the same name.

The snow covered flanks of the Lune Gorge provide a Christmas card setting for No. 86207 *City of Lichfield* hauling the 06.00 Aberdeen-Birmingham New Street service through Grayrigg, near Shap, on 9th February 1983.

124.
Heading south through Tamworth on 25th August 1980, No. 86218 *Planet* powers what is thought to be the slightly late-running 13.12 from Manchester Piccadilly to Euston. Without the advantage of route indicator panels, certain identification of a train from lineside is not always possible.

Gavin Morrison

125.
At Manchester on a wet 1st June 1984, an ex-Glasgow 'Blue Train' electric unit, Class 303 No. 303041, leaves the Oxford Road platforms forming the 13.22 Crewe-Altrincham service with a Class 304 emu in the background with a train for Alderley Edge. In the Piccadilly platform No. 86247 *Abraham Darby* awaits departure time with the 14.15 to Euston.

126 & 127.
To commemorate the 150th Anniversary of the Liverpool & Manchester Railway in 1980, two Class 86 locomotives which carried the names of contenders in the Rainhill trials were given a special livery that included the coat of arms of the L&MR. No. 86214 *Sans Pareil* (above) accelerates away from Crewe station on 16th August 1981 with a Blackpool-Euston service, while No. 86235 *Novelty* (below) passes Basford Hall Junction on 30th October 1980 with the 13.00 train from Holyhead to Euston.

Both: Barry J. Nicolle

128.
Smartly attired in InterCity Sector livery, No. 86212 *Preston Guild* fairly hurtles through Berkhamsted station on 21st February 1987 at the head of the 14.30 service from Euston to Liverpool Lime Street.

129.
With mainly matching coaching stock of InterCity Sector livery, No. 86234 *J B Priestley O.M.* travels between Harrow & Wealdstone and Kenton on 28th June 1987 heading the 09.00 Wolverhampton-Euston train. The additional front end fitments relate to driver/guard communication and also incorporate a facility for 'push-pull' working as required. The system is known as Time Division Multiplex (TDM).

130.
Bathed in sunshine outside Willesden depot on 7th September 1987, the InterCity Sector livery of No. 86217 *Halley's Comet* contrasts with the plain 'rail blue' of first-generation AC electric locomotives Nos 81006 and 85010. Originally named *Comet* in October 1980, No. 86217 was re-named in November 1985 to commemorate the reappearance of the famous comet.

131.
Inside Willesden depot on the same day, No. 86231 *Starlight Express* displays a different style of InterCity livery with the dark grey upper section having been extended around the front end. No. 86406, on the adjacent line, has the standard version of this paintwork. Both locomotives have been fitted with TDM and a headlight.

Class 86/3

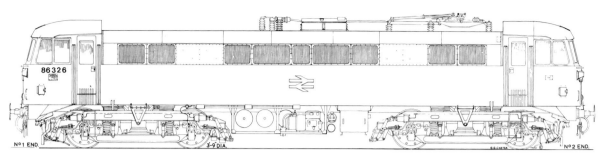

Drawing P
Class 86/3 No. 86326 showing the 'A' side.

132.
With a large number of the total Class 86 fleet being restricted to duties that did not entail a top speed of more than 80 mph, there was a resultant shortage of motive power for the sustained high-speed running required for the West Coast Main Line InterCity timetable. In order to provide another 20 locomotives capable of 100 mph timings, this number of Class 86/0s were fitted with SAB resilient wheels as an interim measure from 1980, but were not converted with new 'Flexicoil' suspension until much later. This short-lived sub-class was classified 86/3 with all of them now converted to 86/4. On 2nd June 1984, No. 86319 (now 86419) pulls away after the scheduled Stoke-on-Trent stop with the 14.15 Manchester Piccadilly-Euston service.

133.
Having been fitted for multiple-unit working when classified 86/0, No. 86320 (now 86420) retains the facility and here backs on to the 09.50 Paddington-Liverpool Lime Street train at Birmingham New Street on 5th March 1953. The train had been hauled this far by Class 50 diesel-electric Co-Co No. 50006 *Neptune.* At the opposite platform the 07.25 Penzance-Edinburgh InterCity 125 service is headed by Class 254 Power Car No. 43180.

134.
On 2nd February 1985, Hertfordshire Railtours "Great Eastern Pullman" special hauled by No. 86324 (now 86424) nears Great Bentley, on the Clacton Line. The coaching stock is from the "Manchester Pullman" which it had hauled from Southend with a reversal at Shenfield.

Michael J. Collins

135.
The 09.50 InterCity service from Euston to Manchester Piccadilly whistles through Macclesfield station on 2nd June 1984 powered by No. 86319 (now 86419).

136.
With the electrical current between Euston and Willesden being switched off to enable engineering work to take place inside Primrose Hill Tunnel on Sunday, 1st April 1984, all electrically powered stock had to be diesel hauled to and from the terminus. This was in the hands of Classes 25 and 31/1 from Cricklewood depot. Ecs of the "Royal Highlander" sleeping car service is dragged up Camden Bank by Class 25/2 Bo-Bo No. 25218 with the pantograph on No. 86313 (now 86413 *County of Lancashire)* switched down. The Class 25 has since been withdrawn from service.

137.
Engineering work to the overhead catenary necessitated diesel haulage from Stafford on Sunday, 15th February 1981 with Class 47/4 Co-Co No. 47515 hauling No. 86317 (now 86417 *The Kingsman),* and the stock that made up the 10.50 service from Euston to Liverpool Lime Street.

Graham Scott-Lowe

Class 86/4

138.
The sub-division classification 86/4 is made up of original condition Class 86/0 locomotives fitted with SAB resilient wheels and 'Flexicoil' suspension, plus the 20 Class 86/3 machines that had already received SAB wheels, but were also now modified with the revised suspension. Externally there is no appreciable difference between the Class 86/2 and 86/4 but they retain their different sub-division categories as all the Part 4s are fitted for multiple working and retain the original 282AZ traction motors, Class 86/2 utilising type 282BX. On 16th September 1987, No. 86403 races through Cheddington with the 15.50 ''Merseyside Pullman'' from Euston to Liverpool Lime Street and, despite the very dull weather conditions prevailing at the time, assists in brightening the scene a little with locomotive and stock all in matching InterCity Sector livery.

139.
Between Leighton Buzzard and Cheddington on the same day, No. 86421 *London School of Economics* has charge of the 14.30 Manchester Piccadilly-Euston express and was travelling at near to 100 mph when this photograph was taken. Both this locomotive and the one shown above are using the Brecknell Willis 'Highspeed' pantograph.

140.
On Bank Holiday Monday, 31st August 1987, insect-bespattered No. 86415 *Rotary International* reaches the end of the 25kV AC overhead electrification at Mitre Bridge Junction, Willesden, and is detached from the 10.30 Liverpool Lime Street-Dover Western Docks cross-London InterCity service. Class 47/4 diesel Co-Co No. 47613 *North Star* waits to take over the train for the remainder of the journey, most of which will take place over Southern Region third-rail territory.

141.
The 10.50 Sunday service from Euston to Liverpool Lime Street hares through Kenton, Middlesex, on 28th June 1987 with No. 86425 providing traction. Resplendent in InterCity Sector livery with sealed beam headlamp, marker lights and the Time Division Multiplex fitting in addition to a 'Highspeed' pantograph, 'Flexicoil' suspension and resilient wheels, this locomotive is barely recognisable from the original No. E3186 of Type AL6 which appeared new from Vulcan Foundry in November 1965.

142 & 143.
To inaugurate the extension of electrification on the ex-Great Eastern line to Cambridge, a special train was run from Liverpool Street station on 23rd March 1987 behind No. 86401 which had been specially painted for the occasion in the startling red, white, blue and grey livery of the Network SouthEast Sector. After a record-breaking run of 47 minutes from start to stop, the locomotive (above) brings the empty stock for the return trip into Cambridge station and (below) is seen on arrival at the London terminus.

144.
With just 28 miles to go before reaching Euston, the 11.33 service from Shrewsbury passes Berkhamsted on 21st February 1987 hauled by No. 86401. Nameplates *The Chartered Institute of Transport* have been allocated to this locomotive but have yet to be fitted.

145.
On 17th September 1987, two Class 86/4s engage in multiple working with a down Freightliner service from Willesden passing Dudswell, south of Tring, in Hertfordshire. The Network SouthEast livery of No. 86401 contrasts markedly with the InterCity colours of No. 86419.

Ken Brunt

146 & 147.
Twenty one years of the name InterCity being used to market British Rail's premier express services was celebrated during the Spring of 1987 and one of the many events that took place was a reconstruction of the ''Merseyside Express' of 1966. Hauling all-maroon stock complete with coachboards, locomotive No. 86426 was returned to as near original appearance as possible with an application of 'electric blue' paint with raised old-style BR logo and original number E3195. The locomotive is seen at Euston station on 1st May (above) awaiting the 'off' following considerable attention from the media, and (below) sets out on the journey to Liverpool Lime Street with invited guests and passes Class 85 No. 85014 which is stabled outside the station awaiting the next duty.

148.
Approaching Crewe station on 9th April 1987, No. 86438 slows for the obligatory stop with the 10.15 train from Dover Western Docks to Liverpool Lime Street, one of the cross-London InterCity services which were introduced in May of the previous year.

149.
On 21st February 1987, No. 86402 scampers through attractive Hertfordshire countryside between Northchurch Tunnel and Berkhamsted powering the 09.56 InterCity service from Wolverhampton to Euston. With the remainder of the Class 86/4 fleet carrying Sector colours, this particular locomotive was, rather strangely, outshopped in the old-style 'rail blue' following modification from Class 86/0 No. 86002.

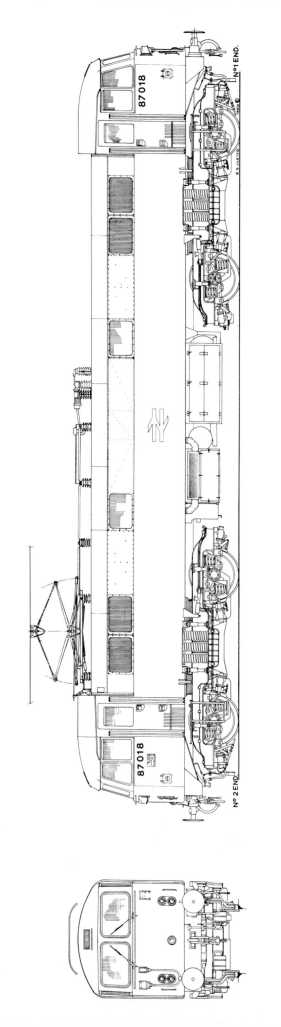

Drawing Q.
Class 87 No. 87018 as constructed in 1973 – 'B' side.

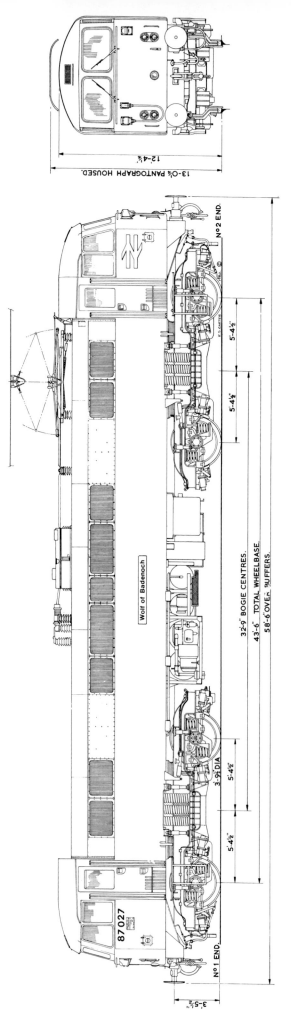

Drawing R.
Class 87 No. 87027 *Wolf of Badenoch* as named in 1978 – 'A' side.

Class 87/0

Designed specifically for the 25kV AC electrification extension through to Glasgow in 1974, building of the fleet of 36 Class 87 locomotives began at Crewe Works in June 1972 with the first being delivered one year later. Geared to reach 110 mph, they were suitable for high-speed operation but were otherwise of a standard design that was compatible with the existing first and second generation AC electric locomotives of Classes 81 to 86. To improve riding qualities, the GEC412AZ traction motors were frame-mounted and 'Flexicoil' suspension was standard. Other differences from earlier designs included windscreens formed of two panels instead of three, no panel for the train reporting number, the fitting of a fixed beam headlight, a single GEC cross-arm pantograph and the ability to work only air-braked trains, previous types being then dual-braked. All were capable of multiple unit working, were fitted with sanding gear and, like Classes 85 and 86, were capable of having the upper portion of the roof section between the cabs completely removed for ease of access during heavy maintenance. The bodysides were also similar to the Class 86 with a bank of nine louvre grilles fitted to the 'A' side and four grilles and two windows being contained on the 'B' side. Apart from a few initial minor problems with the traction motors and wheel sets, the Class 87s have been more or less trouble free since their introduction and, apart from five of the fleet having a short spell of two months allocated to Glasgow Shields Road in 1974, all have been maintained at Willesden depot throughout.

150.
The 10.45 Euston-Glasgow Central, the famous "Royal Scot" express, is seen here at speed through Bushey on 29th April 1978 powered by Class 87/0 No. 87021. British Rail having decided to resume a naming policy for their more important locomotives, the Class 87 fleet became one of the first recipients for nameplates, this example becoming *Robert the Bruce*, just over five weeks after this photograph was taken.

151.

Above: The Class 87 was the first fleet of AC electric locomotives to be constructed at BREL Crewe. This view of the production line dates from early 1973 and shows, from left to right, Nos 87004, 87005 and 87001 in various stages of the build. Taking the form of a single longitudinal box section assembly, the body underframe is fabricated by welding and constructed integrally from steel plate and folded sections. The removable roof section between the cabs can be clearly seen in this view.

Colin J. Marsden collection

153.

Right top: Shortly after the introduction of electric working through to Glasgow, No. 87025 appears to treat the undulations of the Shap Fell terrain with complete disdain, and is here travelling at close to 90 mph with the 07.45 Euston-Glasgow Central express on 12th June 1974. This locomotive was given the name *Borderer* in 1978 but was subsequently renamed *County of Cheshire* at Crewe station in November 1982.

152.

Below: With the yellow front end below the cab windows almost blackened by a multitude of dead insects, No. 87032 races through Hatch End in Middlesex on 30th June 1973 in charge of the 08.59 Wolverhampton-Euston service. It would be nearly five years before the nameplates *Kenilworth* were bestowed.

154.
Below: Just under two months prior to being named, the large, centrally placed bodyside BR logos on No. 87015 have been removed in order to make way for *Howard of Effingham* plates, smaller logos having been painted on opposite cabsides. On 18th March 1978, the locomotive moves away from Birmingham New Street station with the 12.05 InterCity service for Edinburgh and Glasgow and clearly illustrates the uncluttered roof of the Class 87.

155.
On a cloudless 30th June 1976, No. 87020 storms through Bushey with the 08.45 Euston-Glasgow Central express. Being fitted only for haulage of air-braked stock, the Class 87 fleet was initially precluded from working many freight duties and, in consequence, their maximum availability for operations was somewhat restricted. This locomotive was named *North Briton* in May 1978.

156.
On 5th January 1975, No. 87006 draws to a halt at Coventry station with the 10.40 Euston-Wolverhampton service. Named *City of Glasgow* in December 1977, the plates were changed to read *Glasgow Garden Festival* during 1987 but are scheduled to revert back when the festival is over.

157.
Appropriately hauled by No. 87007 *City of Manchester,* the 13.12 from Manchester Piccadilly to Euston takes the fast road through Rugeley station on 19th June 1980. Although geared for 110 mph running, track conditions were not considered suitable for the class to travel at speeds above 100 mph until the summer timetables of 1984 when new high speed pantographs were also fitted.

John Vaughan

158.
With the coaching stock made up of seven Mk 3s led by one Mk 2 and with a BG (gangwayed brake) bringing up the rear, the 14.50 Euston-Manchester Piccadilly InterCity express approaches Rugeley at speed on the same day, powered by No. 87027 *Wolf of Badenoch.*

John Vaughan

159.
Left: With eight of the nine coaches labelled 'InterCity', the 17.20 Edinburgh-Birmingham New Street express appears to glide effortlessly towards Beattock Summit, near Crawford in Lanarkshire, on 4th May 1980 with No. 87002 *Royal Sovereign* at the working end. All the equipment fitted to the Class 87 fleet was provided by GEC Traction Ltd.

John S. Whiteley

160.
Above: Hest Bank station closed in February 1969. On the downhill stretch of line near the old station site, north of Lancaster on 8th February 1983, No. 87021 *Robert the Bruce* passes a caravan site with the 12.45 express from Euston to Glasgow Central. The caravans are not as strangely placed as one may think from this view, as the other side of the area overlooks Morecambe Bay!

161.
Below: Sweeping downgrade through Grayrigg, near Shap, on 9th February 1983, No. 87023 *Highland Chieftain* has charge of the 07.45 London-bound express from Glasgow Central. The title ''Highland Chieftain'' having been given to an Inverness High Speed Train service from King's Cross, the plates affixed here were removed in May 1984 and the name given to InterCity 125 power car No. 43092. The Class 87 now carries the name *Velocity*.

162.
Left: With Class 45/0 'Peak' 1Co-Co1 diesel-electric No. 45017 stabled in the opposite platform, No. 87014 *Knight of the Thistle* speeds through Nuneaton station on 27th March 1982 powering the 09.12 express from Manchester Piccadilly to Euston.

163.
Centre left: Leaving Glasgow Central station on a sunny evening in May 1978, No. 87034 *William Shakespeare* commences a journey of over 400 miles with the 17.30 service for London Euston.

Colin Boocock

164.
Bottom left: Two onlookers keep wisely behind the yellow platform lines that warn of high speed trains, as No. 87017

Iron Duke hurtles through Milton Keynes station on 6th October 1984 with the early running 10.00 Liverpool Lime Street-Euston express.

165.
Below: Swinging the camera with the subject at speed, in order to produce a blurred backround and the resultant impression of movement, is not an easy pursuit and one that is even more difficult when perpetrated with a telephoto lens. Using this technique, the photographer has succeeded very well in capturing No. 87015 *Howard of Effingham* travelling through Willesden with a northbound express and has also provided a good illustration of the double door locks and handles that are fitted to the Class 87 fleet.

Ken Brunt

166.

In May 1984, two Class 87 locomotives were experimentally repainted in new colours at Willesden depot, No. 87006 *City of Glasgow* appearing in dark grey with large BR logos and numbers and No. 87012 *Coeur de Lion* emerging in what has become the standard livery for the InterCity Sector as illustrated in the other three photographs on these pages. The paintwork on No. 87006 was short lived and was soon replaced with the same colours as sported by No. 87012. Prior to this occurring, however, the machine was photographed at the buffer stops in Manchester Piccadilly station on 1st June 1984 after a very late arrival with the 11.50 service from Euston brought about by braking problems en route.

167.
Below left: Rounding the curve through Berkamsted on 21st February 1987, No. 87001 *Royal Scot* races northwards with the 13.45 express for Glasgow Central. This machine originally carried the name *Stephenson* which was transferred to the bodysides of the Class 87/1 locomotive No. 87101 in 1977. Observe the Brecknell Willis 'Highspeed' pantograph and the 'Time Division Multiplex' fitment on either side of the headlight, both of which are now standard for the class.

168.
Above: Fresh from Crewe Works, No. 87006, with temporary *Glasgow Garden Festival* nameplates, sprints through Kenton on 20th November 1987 with the ''Royal Scot'' express for Glasgow Central. Matching InterCity Sector livery on both locomotive and stock, gives this prestige train a very impressive appearance.

169.
Below: On 9th April 1987, newly renamed No. 87014 *Velocity* takes the fast road through Crewe station with the 13.45 Euston-Glasgow Central express as Class 47/0 Co-Co diesel-electric No. 47193 hauls empty hoppers southwards. Compared with the other two examples on these pages, the executive grey portion of the InterCity Sector livery on the Class 87 has not been continued around the front of the locomotive.

Class 87/1

The final locomotive of the Class 87 build was to have been numbered 87036 but as it contained a number of experimental features including thyristor control, it was designated as Class 87/1 and subsequently numbered 87101. The locomotive emerged from Crewe Works in early 1975 but remained in restricted service under test by the Research Department at Derby as it was thought that the thyristor equipment would interfere with signals and telecommunications. In the event, this small problem proved to be no worse than that which had already been encountered on the other types of AC electric locomotive and it entered revenue earning service, allocated to Willesden depot in January 1977. The nameplates *Stephenson* were fitted in October 1977 from No. 87001 which was renamed *Royal Scot,* it being decided that the Class 87 fleet would be known as the 'Royal Scot' class but, in fact, the name did not catch on with either railwayman or enthusiast, anymore than the attempt to give the Class 50 diesel fleet the title of 'Warships'. It would seem to be a fact that a class name should be innovative for it to be accepted and not merely a repeat of something that has gone before. Until the advent of the third generation machines of Class 89, 90 and 91, No. 87101 was considered to be the best AC electric locomotive on BR metals with a hauling ability nearly 20 per cent better than a standard Class 87, mainly as a result of thyristor control and separately excited traction motors with better anti-slip characteristics.

170.
On 1st June 1984, Class 87/1 No. 87101 *Stephenson* departs from Manchester Piccadilly station with the 10.15 InterCity service for Euston. Should the advanced thyristor control not be required for any reason, the locomotive will operate as a conventional Class 87/0 merely by the turn of a key.

171.
Basically, a thyristor is a high-speed electrical switch without any moving parts, that can move from low power up to many thousands of kilowatts, providing a very smooth, stepless control and a considerable weight saving advantage over the standard types. This results in reduced maintenance, simpler transformers and a greater hauling capacity, due to there being no tractive effort 'troughs'. Early in its revenue earning career, and shortly after naming, No. 87101 *Stephenson* draws away from Euston station with the 13.10 service for Birmingham New Street.

172.
In the latter part of 1987 and during early 1988, No. 87101 was used quite extensively in connection with evaluation trials for the 'International' train set. Inside Crewe Electric depot on Saturday, 31st October 1987, the locomotive is attached to a Derby Research Department test coach and three 'International' cars ready to recommence work on the following Monday.

Names and Numbers

In order to avoid any confusion with steam engines that were still operative, the numbers of the new British Rail diesel and electric locomotives were given a prefix of D and E respectively. With the introduction of 'Total Operations Processing System' computerisation, or 'TOPS', however, they were all allocated a class number which was incorporated as the first two digits of the new number. Existing AC electric locomotives at the time being identified as Classes 81 to 86 with 87 to 91 following, but omitting the classification 88.

A class 87 was the first AC electric locomotive to receive a name when the plates *Stephenson* were applied by the Stephenson Locomotive Society to No. 87001. Today, the majority of the 86 and 87 fleets have received a name as shown on these pages:-

Class 81

TOPS No.	Original No.
81001	E3001
–	E3002
81002	E3003
81003	E3004
81004	E3005
81005	E3006
81006	E3007
81007	E3008
–	E3009
81008	E3010
81009	E3011
81010	E3012
81011	E3013
81012	E3014
81013	E3015
81014	E3016
81015	E3017
81016	E3018
–	E3019
81017	E3020
81018	E3021
81019	E3022
81020	E3023
81021	E3096
81022	E3097

Class 82

–	E3046
82001	E3047
82002	E3048
82003	E3049
82004	E3050
82005	E3051
82006	E3052
82007	E3053
82008	E3054
–	E3055

Class 83

83001	E3024
83002	E3025
83003	E3026
83004	E3027
83005	E3028
83006	E3029
83007	E3030
83008	E3031
83009	E3032
83010	E3033
83011	E3034
83012	E3035
83013	E3098*
83014	E3099*
83015	E3100**

* Originally carried E3303 & E3304 respectively

**Originally allocated E3305 but not carried

Class 84

84001	E3036
84002	E3037
84003	E3038
84004	E3039
84005	E3040
84006	E3041
84007	E3042
84008	E3043
84009	E3044
84010	E3045

Class 85

85001	E3056
85002	E3057
85003	E3058
85004	E3059
85005	E3060
85006	E3061
85007	E3062
85008	E3063
85009	E3064
85010	E3065
85011	E3066
85012	E3067
85013	E3068
85014	E3069
85015	E3070
85016	E3071
85017	E3072
85018	E3073
85019	E3074
85020	E3075
85021	E3076
85022	E3077
85023	E3078
85024	E3079
85025	E3080
85026	E3081
85027	E3082
85028	E3083
85029	E3084
85030	E3085
85031	E3086
85032	E3087
85033	E3088
85034	E3089
85035	E3090
85036	E3091
85037	E3092
85038	E3093
85039	E3094
85040	E3095

Class 86

86101 (E3191/86201)	*Sir William A Stanier FRS*
86102 (E3150/86202)	*Robert A. Riddles*
86103 (E3143/86203)	*André Chapelon*
86204 (E3173)	*City of Carlisle*
86205 (E3129)	*City of Lancaster*
86206 (E3184)	*City of Stoke on Trent*
86207 (E3179)	*City of Lichfield* (Allocated *City of Chester* but not fitted)
86208 (E3141)	*City of Chester* (Allocated *City of Lichfield* but not fitted)
86209 (E3125)	*City of Coventry*
86210 (E3190)	*City of Edinburgh* (Allocated *Hardwicke*, then *City of Preston* but neither fitted)
86211 (E3147)	*City of Milton Keynes*
86212 (E3151)	*Preston Guild* (allocated *City of Edinburgh* but not fitted)
86213 (E3193)	*Lancashire Witch*
86214 (E3106)	*Sans Pareil* (Allocated *Sanspareil* but amended)
86215 (E3165)	*Joseph Chamberlain* (Allocated *Novelty* but not fitted)
86216 (E3166)	*Meteor* (Allocated *Hardwicke* but not fitted)
86217 (E3177)	*Halley's Comet* (Previously *Comet*)
86218 (E3175)	*Planet*
86219 (E3196)	*Phoenix*
86220 (E3156)	*The Round Tabler* (Previously *Goliath*)
86221 (E3132)	*BBC Look East* (Previously *Vesta*)
86223 (E3158)	*Norwich Union* (Previously *Hector*)
86224 (E3134)	*Caledonian*
86225 (E3164)	*Hardwicke* (Allocated *Lion*, then *Mentor* but neither fitted)
86226 (E3162)	*Royal Mail Midlands* (Previously *Mail*)
86227 (E3117)	*Sir Henry Johnson* (Allocated *Lady of the Lake* but not fitted)
86228 (E3167)	*Vulcan Heritage*
86229 (E3119)	*Sir John Betjeman*
86230 (E3168)	*The Duke of Wellington*
86231 (E3126)	*Starlight Express* (Allocated *Lady of the Lake* but not fitted)
86232 (E3113)	*Harold MacMillan*
86233 (E3172)	*Laurence Olivier*
86234 (E3155)	*J B Priestley O.M.*
86235 (E3194)	*Novelty*
86236 (E3133)	*Josiah Wedgwood*
86237 (E3197)	*Sir Charles Hallé* (Allocated *Arrow* but not fitted)
86238 (E3116)	*European Community* (Allocated *Lord Stamp* but not fitted)

86239 (E3169)		*L.S. Lowry*
86240 (E3127)		*Bishop Eric Treacy*
86241 (E3121)		*Glenfiddich*
86242 (E3138)		*James Kennedy G.C.*
86243 (E3181)		*The Boys' Brigade*
86244 (E3178)		*The Royal British Legion*
86245 (E3182)		*Dudley Castle*
86246 (E3149)		*Royal Anglian Regiment* (Allocated *Scafell Pike* but not fitted)
86247 (E3192)		*Abraham Darby*
86248 (E3107)		*Sir Clwyd/County of Clwyd*
86249 (E3161)		*County of Merseyside*
86250 (E3189)		*The Glasgow Herald*
86251 (E3183)		*The Birmingham Post*
86252 (E3101)		*The Liverpool Daily Post*
86253 (E3136/86044)		*The Manchester Guardian*
86254 (E3142/86047)		*William Webb Ellis*
86255 (E3154/86042)		*Penrith Beacon*
86256 (E3135/86040)		*Pebble Mill*
86257 (E3139/86043)		*Snowdon*
86259 (E3137/86045)		*Peter Pan*
86260 (E3144/86048)		*Driver Wallace Oakes G. C.*
86261 (E3118/86041)		*Driver John Axon G. C.*
86401 (E3199/86001)		*The Chartered Institute of Transport* (Allocated but not fitted).
86402 (E3170/86002)		
86403 (E3115/86003)		
86404 (E3103/86004)		
86405 (E3185/86005)		
86406 (E3112/86006)		
86407 (E3176/86007)		*Institution of Electrical Engineers*
86408 (E3180/86008)		*St John Ambulance*
86409 (E3102/86009)		
86410 (E3104/86010)		
86411 (E3171/86011/86311)		*Airey Neave*
86412 (E3122/86012/86312)		*Elizabeth Garrett Anderson*
86413 (E3128/86013/86313)		*County of Lancashire*
86414 (E3145/86014/86314)		*Frank Hornby*
86415 (E3123/86015/86315)		*Rotary International*
86416 (E3109/86016/86316)		*Wigan Pier*
86417 (E3146/86017/86317)		*The Kingsman*
86418 (E3163/86018/86318)		
86419 (E3120/86019/86319)		
86420 (E3114/86020/86320)		*Royal Mail Midlands* (Allocated but not fitted)
86421 (E3157/86021/86321)		*London School of Economics*
86422 (E3174/86022/86322)		
86423 (E3152/86023/86323)		
86424 (E3111/86024/86324)		
86425 (E3186/86025/86325)		
86426 (E3195/86026/86326)		
86427 (E3110/86027/86327)		*The Industrial Society*
86428 (E3159/86028/86328)		*Aldaniti*
86429 (E3200/86029/86329)		*The Times*
86430 (E3105/86030/86330)		*Scottish National Orchestra*
86431 (E3188/86031)		
86432 (E3148/86032)		*Brookside*
86433 (E3198/86033)		*Wulfruna*
86434 (E3187/86034)		*University of London*
86435 (E3124/86035)		
86436 (E3160/86036)		
86437 (E3130/86037)		
86438 (E3108/86038)		
86439 (E3153/86039)		
86501 (E3140/86046/86258)		*Talyllyn* (Allocated *Ben Nevis* but not fitted)
86502 (E3131/86222)		*Lloyds List* (Previously *Fury*)

Class 87

87001	*Royal Scot* (Original **Stephenson** plates transferred to 87101)
87002	*Royal Sovereign*
87003	*Patriot*
87004	*Britannia*
87005	*City of London*
87006	*Glasgow Garden Festival* (original plates *City of Glasgow* to be restored at completion of festival).
87007	*City of Manchester*
87008	*City of Liverpool*
87009	*City of Birmingham*
87010	*King Arthur*
87011	*The Black Prince*
87012	*Coeur de Lion* (Plates not carried from 1987)
87013	*John O'Gaunt*
87014	*Knight of the Thistle*
87015	*Howard of Effingham*
87016	*Sir Francis Drake* (Name transferred to IC125 Power Car No. 43186)
87017	*Iron Duke*
87018	*Lord Nelson*
87019	*Sir Winston Churchill*
87020	*North Briton*
87021	*Robert the Bruce*
87022	*Cock o'the North*
87023	*Velocity* (Originally *Highland Chieftain* – plates transferred to IC 125 Power Car No. 43092)
87024	*Lord of the Isles*
87025	*County of Cheshire* (Originally *Borderer*)
87026	*Sir Richard Arkwright* (Originally *Redgauntlet*)
87027	*Wolf of Badenoch*
87028	*Lord President*
87029	*Earl Marischal*
87030	*Black Douglas*
87031	*Hal o'the Wynd*
87032	*Kenilworth*
87033	*Thane of Fife*
87034	*William Shakespeare*
87035	*Robert Burns*
87101	*Stephenson* (Plates transferred from No. 87001)

173.
Following the theft of one of the *Coeur de Lion* nameplates from No. 87012, the remaining plate was removed by BR and the locomotive is now one of only two Class 87s to be nameless.

174.
Nameplate of No. 86101 commemorating the Chief Mechanical Engineer of the LMS from 1932-1944, the designer of many famous classes of steam engine to include the 'Princess Royal' and the 'Princess Coronation' Pacifics, the 'Royal Scots', 'Jubilees' and 'Black Fives'.

175.
Named at Liverpool Street station on 11th May 1987, the nameplates of No. 86221 are unusual in that *BBC* is in white with *Look East* in standard silver, both on the usual red background.

176.
Originally named *Comet,* No. 86217 was renamed to commemorate the 1986 return of the celebrated astronomical phenomenon.

177.
The plates on the sides of No. 86421 are surmounted by the School's crest.

178.
The best known of all railway photographers, *Bishop Eric Treacy* is commemorated on the bodysides of No. 86240.

179.
The plates of No. 86501 are much deeper than normal due to the epithet 'The First Preserved Railway' being included within the surround. The Talyllyn Railway's crest is also displayed.

180.
The well known British author *J B Priestley O.M.* is remembered on the bodyside of No. 86234.

181.
It would be nice if this nameplate on No. 86219 commemorated the Phoenix Railway Photographic Circle, whose members, past and present, provided the majority of illustrations for this book but, alas, it merely refers to the legendary bird which arises anew from fire every 500 years!

182.
The 150th Anniversary of the Stockton & Darlington Railway in 1975 prompted the Stephenson Locomotive Society to offer BR special stainless steel nameplates with engraved lettering *Stephenson,* which were originally affixed to No. 87001 but later transferred to 87101.

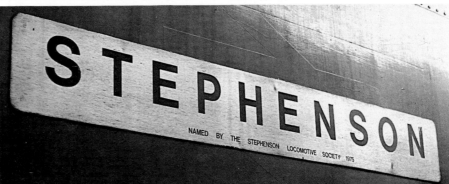

183.
The regimental badge surmounts the plates adorning No. 86246 *Royal Anglian Regiment,* named by HRH The Queen Mother at Liverpool Street in May 1985.

184.
Prior to becoming The Princess Royal, HRH Princess Anne unveils the nameplate *University of London* on No. 86434 at Euston station on 10th April 1986.

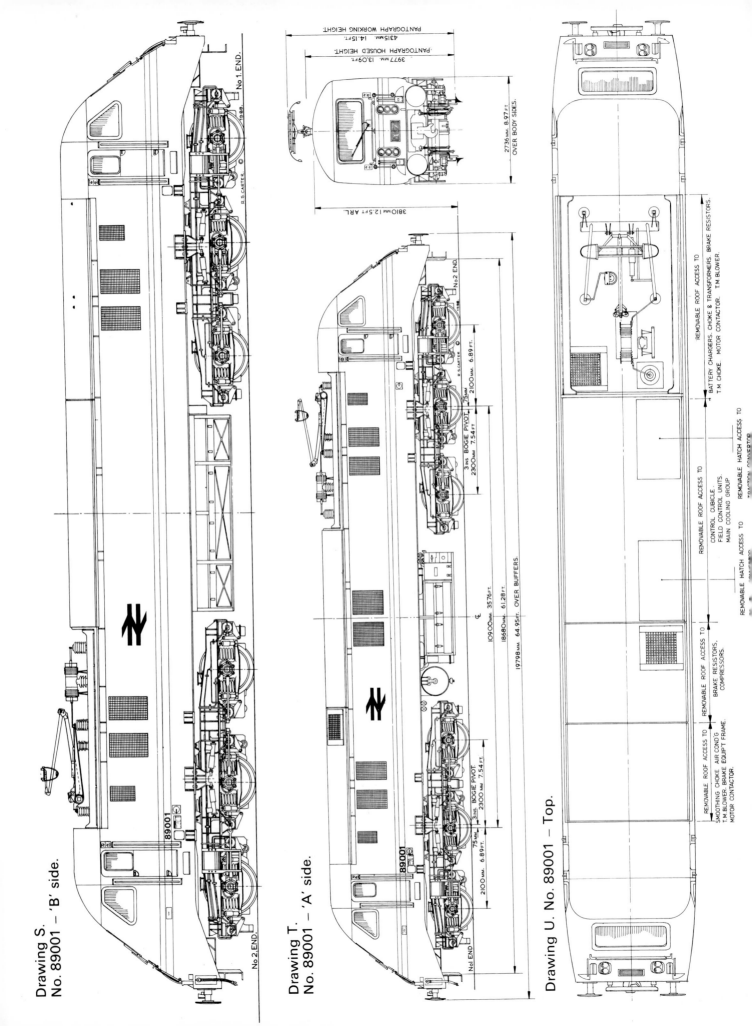

Drawing S.
No. 89001 – 'B' side.

89001

No 1. END.

No 2. END.

Drawing T.
No. 89001 – 'A' side.

89001

No 2 END.

No 1 END.

PANTOGRAPH WORKING HEIGHT.
4315 MM. 14.15 FT.

PANTOGRAPH HOUSED HEIGHT.
3977 MM. 13.09 FT.

2736 MM. 8.97 FT.
OVER BODY SIDES.

3810 MM. 12.5 FT ARL.

75 MM. 3 INS. BOGIE PIVOT 7.54 FT.
2300 MM.

2100 MM. 6.89 FT.

75 MM. 3 INS. BOGIE PIVOT 7.54 FT.
2300 MM.

2100 MM. 6.89 FT.

10900 MM. 35.76 FT. C̄

18680 MM. 61.28 FT.

19798 MM. 64.95 FT. OVER BUFFERS.

Drawing U. No. 89001 – Top.

REMOVABLE ROOF ACCESS TO
BATTERY CHARGERS. CHOKE & TRANSFORMERS. BRAKE RESISTORS.
T.M CHOKE. MOTOR CONTACTOR. T.M. BLOWER.

REMOVABLE ROOF ACCESS TO
CONTROL CUBICLE.
FIELD CONTROL UNITS.
MAIN COOLING GROUP

REMOVABLE HATCH ACCESS TO
TRACTION CONVERTOR.

REMOVABLE ROOF ACCESS TO
BRAKE RESISTORS,
COMPRESSORS.

REMOVABLE ROOF ACCESS TO
SMOOTHING CHOKE AIR COND'G.
T.M. BLOWER. BRAKE EQUIPT FRAME.
MOTOR CONTACTOR.

REMOVABLE HATCH ACCESS TO

Class 89

The single Class 89 locomotive was designed by Brush Electrical Machines Ltd incorporating their own traction equipment with construction undertaken by BREL Crewe, the machine emerging from the Works for evaluation trials in 1986. The locomotive is totally different from any other AC electric type being mounted on Co-Co bogies and incorporating streamlined nose ends reminiscent of the prototype Class 41 High Speed Train. Constructed as a 'production' demonstrator, the Type 89 generates a continuous 5,830hp making it the second most powerful electric locomotive in the country, next to the Class 91. Although principally designed for high speed passenger services, the Co-Co bogie configuration in fact provides a 50% better tractive effort than the Bo-Bo types and could thus eliminate the need for double-heading of locomotives on some freight services that are required to negotiate the formidable Shap and Beattock inclines. For reasons of dynamics, however, BR engineers still favour a Bo-Bo design.

The cab layout of No. 89001 is totally different from the first and second generation AC electric locomotives, having a deep wrap-around desk that incorporates easily observed dials and thoughtfully positioned controls, including speed pre-selection by the driver. A micro-processor based traction control system that also provides automatic fault-logging for maintenance purposes is a feature of the design, and the locomotive is also the first of its kind to be fitted with buckeye couplers. Following trials based from both Derby and Crewe where over 10,000 miles were registered up to October 1987, the Class 89 operated on the East Coast Main Line of the Eastern Region from Hornsey depot in North London prior to being shipped abroad for display at the International Transport & Traffic Exhibition in Hamburg, West Germany in May 1988. In these days of standardisation, its long term future is uncertain, but the Railfreight Sector could take on the machine for long distance 'Speedlink' operations and it is also being looked at very seriously in relation to providing the basis for future motive power for Channel Tunnel services.

185.
The rakish lines of the Class 89 are seen to advantage at this angle, taken at Hornsey depot on 12th December 1987.

186.
Above: No 89001 under construction inside Crewe Works on 25th September 1985.

Colin J. Marsden

187.
Left: Under the auspices of the Derby Technical Centre, the Class 89 receives wind resistance pantograph tests on the Old Dalby test track on 10th April 1987, accompanied by vehicles Nos ADB975-290 *Test Car 6* and ADB975814 *Test Car 10,* all being propelled by Class 47/0 diesel-electric locomotive No. 47235.

Mark Scott

188.
An after dark scene at Crewe on 3rd December 1987 as No. 89001 returns from a test trip to Carlisle.

Ken Brunt

DESIGNED AND SUPPLIED
BY
LOCO N° **BRUSH** 875-1986
BRUSH ELECTRICAL MACHINES LTD
LOUGHBOROUGH ENGLAND ✦ A HAWKER SIDDELEY COMPANY
BUILT BY B.R.E.L. CREWE

189 & 190.
Front end profile of No. 89001 and a close-up of the manufacturer's plate situated below the side cab window.

191.
On 19th January 1988, the Class 89 bursts from Welwyn South Tunnel with the 10.15 Hornsey-Peterborough driver training special. The Brecknell Willis 'Highspeed' pantograph fitted can be clearly seen.

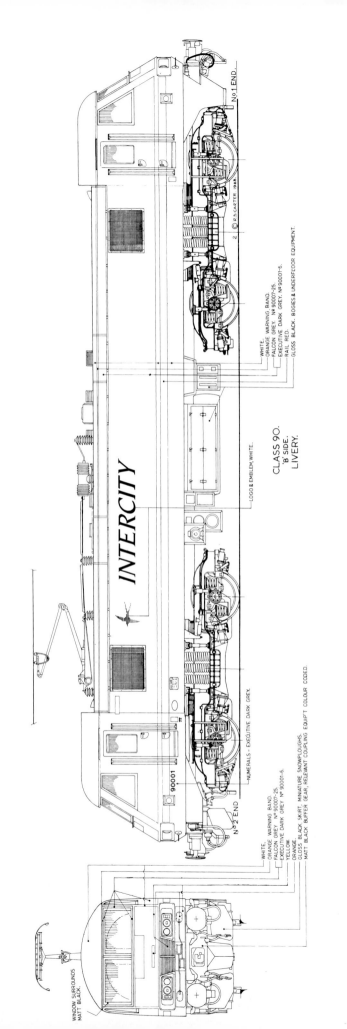

Drawing V.
No. 90001 – 'B' side.

INTERCITY

90001

No 1 END.

No 2 END.

© R.S.CARTER. 1985.

CLASS 90.
'B' SIDE.
LIVERY.

WINDOW SURROUNDS.
MATT BLACK.

WHITE.
ORANGE WARNING BAND.
FALCON GREY. Nº 90007-25.
EXECUTIVE DARK GREY. Nº 90001-6.
RAIL RED.
GLOSS BLACK. BOGIES & UNDERFLOOR EQUIPMENT.

LOGO & EMBLEM. WHITE.

NUMERALS – EXECUTIVE DARK GREY.

WHITE.
ORANGE WARNING BAND.
FALCON GREY. Nº 90007-25.
EXECUTIVE DARK GREY. Nº 90001-6.
YELLOW.
ORANGE BLACK SKIRT, MINIATURE SNOWPLOUGHS.
GLOSS BLACK BUFFER GEAR, RELEVANT COUPLING EQUIP'T COLOUR CODED.
MATT BLACK BUFFER GEAR, RELEVANT COUPLING EQUIP'T COLOUR CODED.

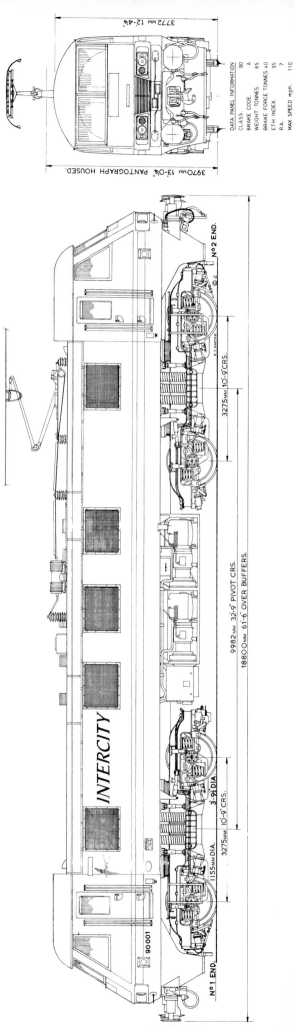

Drawing W.
No. 90001 – 'A' side.

INTERCITY

90001

Nº 1 END.

Nº 2 END.

© R.S.CARTER.

3772mm 12-4⅝"

3970mm 13-0¾" PANTOGRAPH HOUSED.

DATA PANEL INFORMATION
CLASS.   90
BRAKE CODE.   A
WEIGHT TONNES.   85
BRAKE FORCE TONNES.   40
ETH INDEX.   95
RA.   7
MAX SPEED mph.   110

9982mm 32'-9" PIVOT CRS.
18800mm 61'-6" OVER BUFFERS.

3275mm 10'-9"CRS.

3275mm 10'-9"CRS.
3-9½ DIA.
1155mm DIA.

Class 90

Originally to be known as Class 87/2, the 4,850hp Class 90 is a compact Bo-Bo locomotive designed and constructed by British Rail Engineering Ltd (BREL) with GEC electrical equipment. It is destined to become the most important form of traction on the West Coast Main Line from Euston with an initial build of 29 locomotives. A further 21 are scheduled to follow, for operation on freight services and some passenger trains on the East Coast route from King's Cross, running alongside the Class 91s, with four being allocated to the Railfreight Sector for use on the electrified North London line. The Class 90 has similar power equipment to the Class 89 including a computer-based traction control system and also including the same system of speed pre-selection with a maximum of 110 mph. The interior equipment lay-out between the air-conditioned driving compartments is similar to that on the Class 86/87 but air-cooled thyristor converters replace their rectifier modules and provide notchless control of tractive effort. The locomotives are equipped with a remote control system similar to the one used on the Edinburgh-Glasgow push-pull trains using the two lighting wires (known as RCH cables) that are fitted to all passenger carrying coaches on BR up to and including Mk 3 stock. Known as 'Time Division Multiplex' (TDM) it is the same system as fitted to the Class 86/87 and avoids the need for expensive dedicated cables. The fleet will also operate with Mk 4 coaching stock using the twelve-way UIC cables that are fitted to these new vehicles instead of the RCH connections. The Class 90 is able to operate in a similar push-pull manner to the Scottish-based Class 47/7 diesels and will be used in conjunction with new 'Driving Van Trailers' that are styled to match the locomotive on the other end of the new train, a total of 52 such vehicles being constructed by BREL for use on West Coast services. The first Class 90 went from Crewe Works to Derby Technical Centre for trials and evaluation on 31st October 1987 and revenue-earning service followed in 1988.

192.
Although a number of InterCity 125 power cars have been painted in the new-style InterCity Sector livery with swallow motif, introduced in connection with 'InterCity 21' celebrations, No. 90001 was the first actual locomotive to appear in this very smart attire. Note, however, the miniscule locomotive number, particularly as compared with the examples on pictures 126 and 127 or even 145. The BR design team appear to have gone from one extreme to another.

193.
A wooden mock-up of the Class 90 used for initial checking of parts stands in the joiners' shop of BREL Crewe on 9th April 1987.

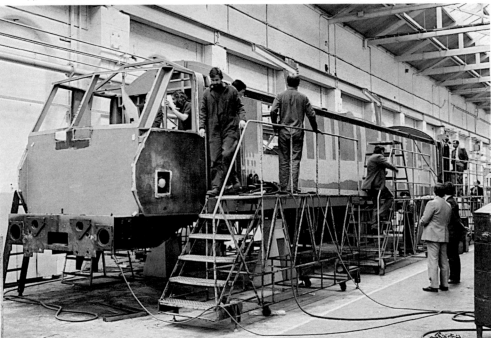

194.
No. 90001 under construction inside Crewe Works on 24th April 1987.

195.
Class 90s Nos 90005 and 90006 take shape at BREL Crewe on 31st October 1987.

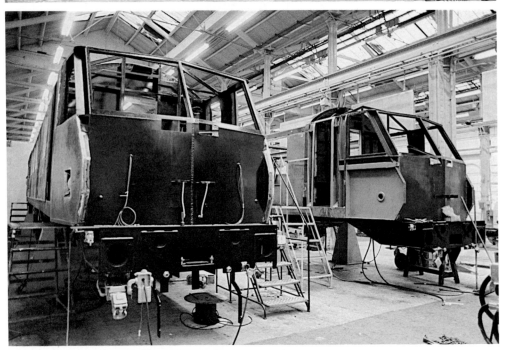

196.
Right: Construction complete, a few final adjustments are made to No. 90001 prior to emerging from the works for the first time. The warning horns can be clearly seen behind the grille between the front lighting banks, with the RCH cables for the TDM system situated below.

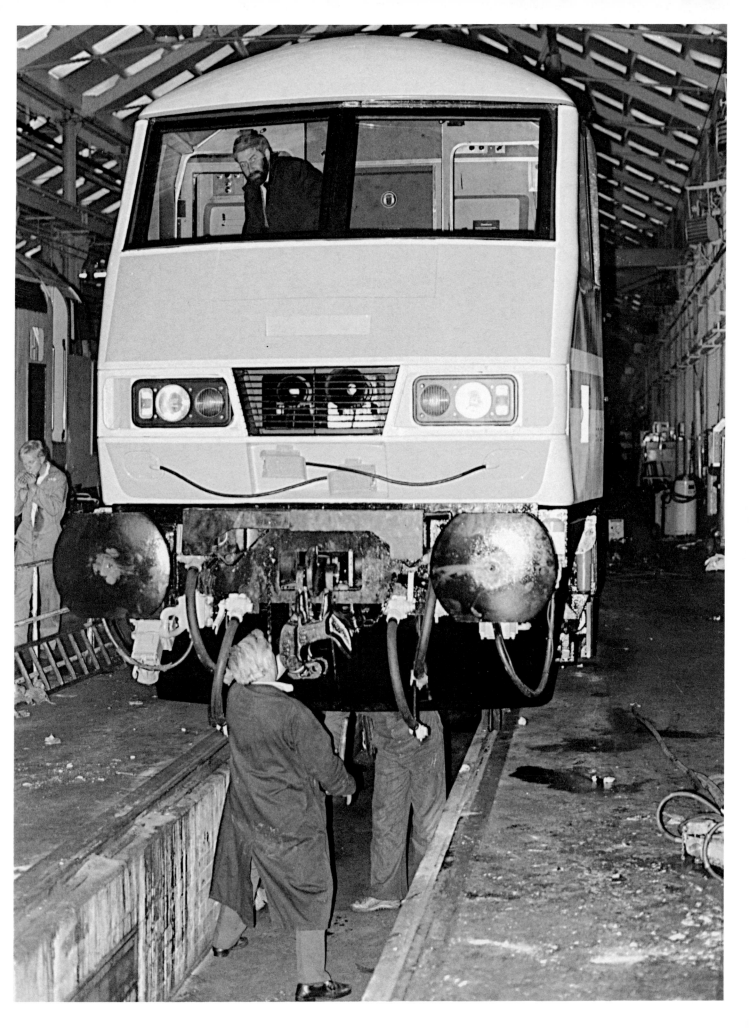

197.
Inside the Derby RTC Engineering Development Unit on 5th November 1987, No. 90001 undergoes static tests attached to test coach No. 975422 *Prometheus*.

Colin J. Marsden

198.
Hauling a test train comprising eight Mk 2 coaches, No. 90003 departs from Crewe station on 16th February 1988 heading for Carlisle via Shap Fell.

John Tuffs

199.
Right: The first Class 90 to receive a name, No. 90005 *Financial Times,* departs from Euston station following the ceremony on 30th March 1988, hauling a Pullman special for Northampton.

200.
Below: On trials, Class 90 No. 90003 passes through Crewe station on 12th February 1988 providing a close-up of the new-style InterCity Sector lettering and motif being applied to the completed locomotives, and also a good view of the Brecknell Willis 'Highspeed' pantograph that is fitted.

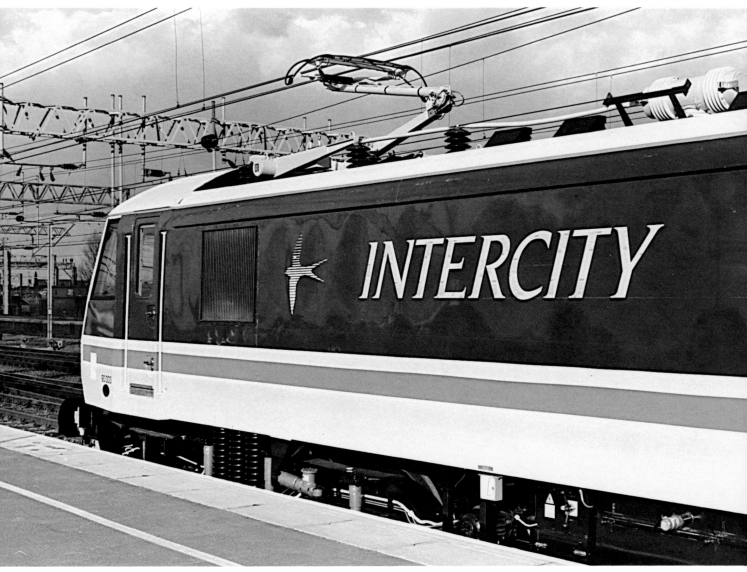

Drawing X.
No. 91001 – 'B' side.

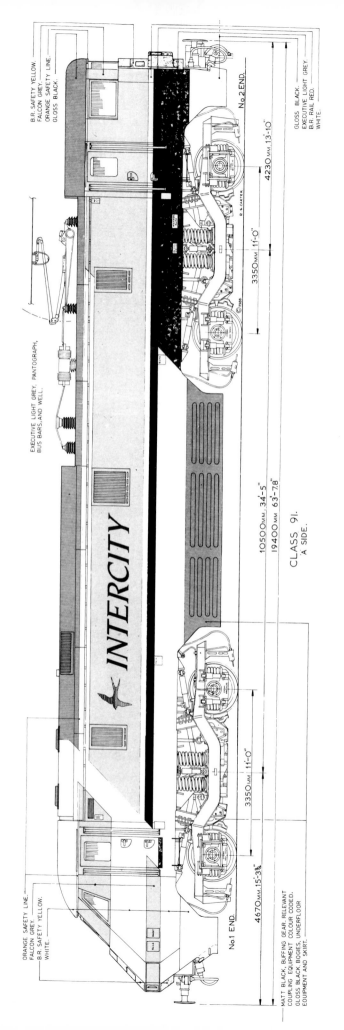

B.R. SAFETY YELLOW.
FALCON GREY.
ORANGE SAFETY LINE.
GLOSS BLACK.

EXECUTIVE LIGHT GREY, PANTOGRAPH,
BUS BARS, AND WELL.

ORANGE SAFETY LINE.
FALCON GREY.
B.R. SAFETY YELLOW.
WHITE.

MATT BLACK, BUFFING GEAR. RELEVANT
COUPLING EQUIPMENT COLOUR CODED.
GLOSS BLACK BOGIES, EQUIPMENT AND SKIRT.
EQUIPMENT AND UNDERFLOOR.

INTERCITY

No 1 END.

4670 MM. 15'-3¼".

3350 MM. 11'-0".

3350 MM. 11'-0".

No 2 END.

4230 MM. 13'-10".

GLOSS BLACK.
EXECUTIVE LIGHT GREY.
B.R. RAIL RED.
WHITE.

10500 MM. 34'-5".

19400 MM. 63'-7.8".

CLASS. 91.
'A' SIDE.

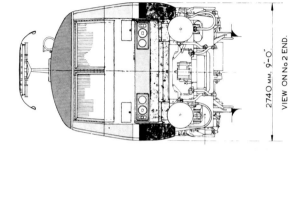

2740 MM. 9'-0".

VIEW ON No 2 END.

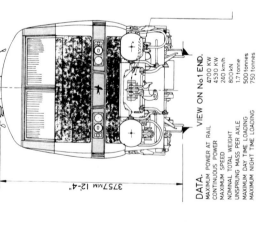

3757 MM 12'-4".

DATA.   VIEW ON No 1 END.
MAXIMUM POWER AT RAIL   4700 KW
CONTINUOUS POWER   4530 KW
MAXIMUM SPEED   240 km/h
MAXIMUM TRACTIVE EFFORT   800 kN
UNSPRUNG MASS PER AXLE   1·7 tonne
MAXIMUM DAY TIME LOADING   500 tonnes
MAXIMUM NIGHT TIME LOADING   750 tonnes

Class 91

Designed by GEC Transportation Projects Ltd and constructed at BREL Crewe with GEC electrical equipment, the Class 91 is the most powerful electric locomotive in the world, providing a continuous 6,080hp with a top speed of 140 mph. Designed to provide high speed services on both the East Coast Main Line between King's Cross and Edinburgh and the West Coast between Euston and Glasgow, the 31 locomotives ordered have the usual two cabs, but one is streamlined and one is not. On normal passenger duty it is expected that the streamlined cab will always be at the end of the train, pulling in one direction and propelling in the other, with the 'blunt' end leading only when the locomotives are involved with overnight sleeper services, freight, or other trains with speed limitations.

Separately excited (Sepex) traction motors are mounted below the body in the space where they would normally be found had they been bogie mounted. This has permitted a conventional equipment lay-out to be achieved within the body which, by locating the main transformer below it as well, has achieved a low centre of gravity to minimise body roll and relative pantograph movement, which is also assisted by means of an anti-roll bar fitted across the secondary suspensions.

The micro-processor control is similar to that provided by GEC for the Class 90 and includes the same self-diagnostic fault facility to assist maintenance. The computer will also ensure good load sharing between individual traction motors and bogie groups with bogie-weight compensation in addition to wheel slip detection and correction, wheel creep control in conjunction with track speed measurement made by GEC Marconi doppler radar, automatic speed limitation, protection against over or under-voltage and over-load should line voltage fluctuate. It will also interface with the TDM system as well as with the air brake system, the various safety provisions and the train tilt controls.

The first locomotive, No. 91001, emerged from Crewe Works for media examination on 12th February 1988 with formal acceptance by BR of the first ten of the class being scheduled for August 1988 when evaluation testing and driver training will be undertaken for the following twelve months, prior to commencing revenue earning on the King's Cross-Leeds services in October 1989; the remainder taking trains through to Edinburgh by May 1991.

201.
Unveiled to the media for the first time on 12th February 1988, the impressive lines of No. 91001 are displayed in Crewe Works yard, just two days before travelling to Derby for the first tests to be carried out at the Research and Development Centre.

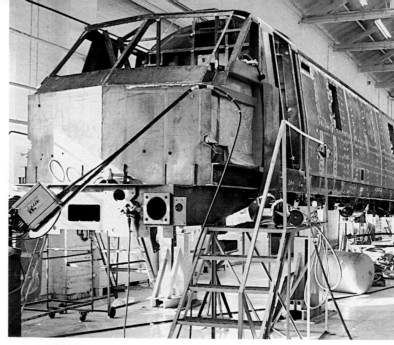

202.
Class 91s Nos 91004 and 91005 take shape inside Crewe Works in February 1988.

203.
The second of the Class 91 fleet nears completion at BREL Crewe on the same day. A view of the 'blunt' end under construction.

204.
The locomotive viewed from the opposite end on the same day.

205 & 206.
Displayed in Crewe yard shortly after having been 'rolled out' for media examination, the 'blunt' end of No. 91001 appears quite conventionally mundane compared with the rather futuristic streamlined end.

207.
Prior to being rolled out into the February sunshine, the completed No. 91001 is seen inside the BREL Works at Crewe on 12th February 1988. For the occasion 'GEC' has been painted onto the buffers.

208.
Few will deny that the streamlined end of the Class 91 is very impressive but, in reality, it is the remarkable technology within the machine which really makes it a product of the modern age. The cab instruments controlling the locomotive surround the driver and the well planned lay-out is more or less the same as can be seen in the Class 89 and the Class 90. This is a view of the driver's controls in the cab of the 'blunt' end but the cab in the streamlined end, is in fact identical.

Anglia Region Operations

209 & 210.
The first driver training run of an AC electric locomotive on the ex-Great Eastern Railway metals from Liverpool Street station, took place on 29th October 1984, when Class 86/3 No. 86316 (now 86416) *Wigan Pier* travelled from Thornton Fields sidings to Colchester and back. Seen above on the outward run, the train is passing Brentwood station on the climb to Ingrave Summit while below, it makes the return journey through Stratford, in East London.

211.
A Norwich-Liverpool Street InterCity express is taken across the River Stour at Manningtree on 6th August 1985, powered by Class 86/2 No. 86239 *L.S. Lowry*.

John Broughton

212.
On the same day, another Class 86/2, No. 86244 *The Royal British Legion* emerges from Ipswich Tunnel into Ipswich station with one of the hourly InterCity services to Norwich from London, Liverpool Street.

John Broughton

213.
On a particularly bright 11th October 1986, No. 86223 *Hector,* hauling the 10.34 InterCity express from Norwich to Liverpool Street, brakes for the required Colchester call, from where the train is scheduled to run non-stop to its destination. *Hector* lost his name during 1987, becoming *Norwich Union* at a ceremony on Norwich station on 1st December 1987.

214.
Passing the very old level crossing keeper's hut at Slipe Lane crossing, Wormley, Hertfordshire, between Cheshunt and Broxbourne on 16th September 1987, Class 86/2 No. 86205 *City of Lancaster* hauls the 14.35 from Liverpool Street to Norwich.

215.
On diversion due to engineering works at London Fields, No. 86247 *Abraham Darby* passes Seven Sisters in North London, with the 09.00 King's Lynn-Liverpool Street service on 12th December 1987. The first and fifth coaches are in Network SouthEast Sector livery.

216.
Top: With the upper half of the locomotive bodysides painted in an experimental dark chocolate brown, instead of the standard 'executive grey' InterCity Sector livery that is shown on the coaching stock, the 10.55 Norwich-Liverpool Street express passes between Seven Kings and Ilford stations on 23rd October 1987, headed by No. 86228 *Vulcan Heritage.*

217.
Above: At the same location and on the same day, but with the camera facing in the opposite direction, No. 86207 *City of Lichfield* passes the back gardens of a part of Essex suburbia. Making light of the 12.30 InterCity service from Liverpool Street to Norwich, it is scheduled to arrive at Norfolk's county town in exactly two hours from London, with calls at Colchester, Manningtree, Ipswich, Needham Market, Stowmarket and Diss.

218.
Not another new numbering scheme, but an instance where a combination of carriage washer and the elements have removed three number transfers from the cabside of what should be No. 86210 *City of Edinburgh,* seen on arrival at Liverpool Street station on 23rd March 1987 with the 07.30 train from Norwich.

219.

Opposite: A 300mm telephoto lens compresses the jungle of overhead catenary and gives the impression that the 1 in 140 gradient approaching Colchester station from the east is more severe than it really is. The candy-stripe effect of alternating liveries on the coaching stock is also emphasised as a boat train from Harwich Parkeston Quay surges through the station, non-stop for Liverpool Street on 11th October 1986 powered by No. 86253 *The Manchester Guardian.* The single line branching off to the right leads to Clacton and Walton-on-Naze.

220.

Above: With pantograph riding high, No.86208 *City of Chester* with the 15.30 express from Liverpool Street to Norwich, draws to a halt for the scheduled Manningtree stop on 5th May 1987.

221.

Left: The first AC electric locomotive to appear on ex-London. Tilbury & Southend Railway lines was No. 86235 *Novelty,* towed in from Stratford Major Depot overnight on 16th October 1987 as a static exhibit for the Ripple Lane Open Day.

222.
Passing Cambridge with a driver-training special, prior to full electric services commencing through to Cambridge, No. 86228 *Vulcan Heritage* heads southwards on 23rd March 1987.

223.
Arriving at Manningtree station on 8th September 1987, the 15.40 Norwich-Liverpool Street InterCity service has No. 86236 *Josiah Wedgwood* providing traction. The train was required to wait for potential passengers for nearly five minutes due to early running.

224.
Prior to electrification being completed through to Norwich, it was necessary for an electric locomotive hauling passenger services from Liverpool Street to come off the train at Ipswich, where Class 47/4 diesel power would be used to continue the journey. On 7th January 1987, No. 86204 *City of Lancaster* is uncoupled from the 13.30 Liverpool Street-Norwich train in order for No. 47585 *County of Cambridgeshire* to take over. In the station yard to the rear can be seen a Class 150/1 'Sprinter' dmu and a Class 101 Metro-Cammell dmu, together with Class 31/1 and 37/0 diesel locomotives.

225.
At dusk on 19th February 1988, No. 86256 *Pebble Mill* prepares to leave Cambridge station with the 17.05 service for Liverpool Street. On the left, Class 305 emus Nos 305515 and 305519 form the 17.27 stopping train to the same destination.

On Great Northern Metals

226
On 2nd November 1986, Class 87/1 No. 87101 *Stephenson* passes Welham Green, near Hatfield, hauling 20 HEA hoppers on a crew-training trip from King's Cross to Hitchin. This was the first occasion that an AC electric locomotive visited King's Cross. Later in the month the wagons were replaced by eight Mk 1 coaches and *Stephenson* gave way to a Class 86/2 which continued the trials.

Ken Brunt

227.
On Easter Monday, 4th April 1988, Class 91 No. 91002 rounds the Hertford Loop between Bowes Park and Alexandra Palace, hauling displaced Mk 3 'sleeper' stock during evaluation trials and driver training between Bounds Green depot and Peterborough. The locomotive is travelling 'blunt end' forward.

228.
Another milestone with the East Coast Main Line electrification took place on 11th November 1987 when the first ever electrically hauled freight train arrived at Peterborough from Willesden, where it had traversed the newly-electrified portion of the North London line. Conveying two Lakeland Pullman coaches for Speedlink customers and the media, in addition to the varied selection of modern freight vehicles, the train passes Fletton, Peterborough, powered by Class 85 No. 85011, the first AC electric locomotive to run under its own power to Peterborough.

Murray Brown

229.
Due to a shortage of suitable electric multiple units on the evening of 11th December 1987, the 16.35 King's Cross-Peterborough service surprisingly consisted of Class 86/4 No. 86403, two 'Motorail' allocated 'open first' coaches and the eight-coach 'West Highland Line' set painted in green and cream! Apart from the unusual stock, this was the first occasion that an electric locomotive worked a timetabled passenger train from King's Cross.

Scenes on Depot

230.
Situated to the north of Crewe station on the Chester route, Crewe Electric Depot is on the opposite side of the line to Crewe Works. Occupants on 31st October 1987 consisted mainly of the Class 85s, all of which are allocated here, although also in attendance was one Class 86/2, the 87/1 and the Research & Development 'load bank' ex-Class 84.

231.
On 25th February 1984, just three of the many locomotives always resident at Willesden depot in North-West London, face towards the Capital in echelon. No. 87001 *Royal Scot* (with the distinctively low number placement carried until being repainted in InterCity Sector livery), No. 87020 *North Briton* and No. 86328 (now 86428 *Aldaniti*).

232.
The large carriage sidings adjacent to Stonebridge Park station in Middlesex, where recently renumbered 85039 is seen on 26th June 1973, were known for many years as Brent yard or Willesden sidings, but in 1987 received the rather grand new title of Wembley InterCity Depot.

233 & 234.
Inside Ilford depot on 23rd October 1987 and 2nd March 1988, respectively, Class 86/2s Nos 86214 *Sans Pareil* and 86227 *Sir Henry Johnson* are 'spare engine' for the Liverpool Street-Cambridge/Norwich services, in the event of any locomotive failure.

235 & 236.
Constructed over 25 years apart, the three-quarter profiles of Classes 82 and 89, both in InterCity Sector livery, make a fascinating contrast at Willesden and Hornsey depots respectively. It is not a new type of pantograph protruding from the rear of the Class 89 but a Hornsey floodlighting standard in the background!

St Pancras Special

237 & 238.
In deference to the Poet Laureate's well known appreciation of the magnificent St Pancras station train shed, 24th June 1983 was the only recorded instance of an AC electric locomotive making an appearance there. The occasion was the naming of Class 86/2 No. 86229 *Sir John Betjeman* by the great man himself. *Above:* Following completion of the ceremonies, the locomotive prepares to leave the station with a special for Bedford and *Below:* It returns later in the day, the SLOA Pullman coaches being utilised in both directions.

In Company

240.
Two Sentinel 4-wheel diesel hydraulic locomotives (Nos 10159 and 10264) belonging to the Tunnel Cement (Pitstone) Ltd shunt wagons and tanks in their BR-connected private sidings at Pitstone, near Tring, on 16th September 1987. Flashing past in the background, Class 87/0 No. 87001 *Royal Scot* powers the 15.31 InterCity service from Shrewsbury to Euston.

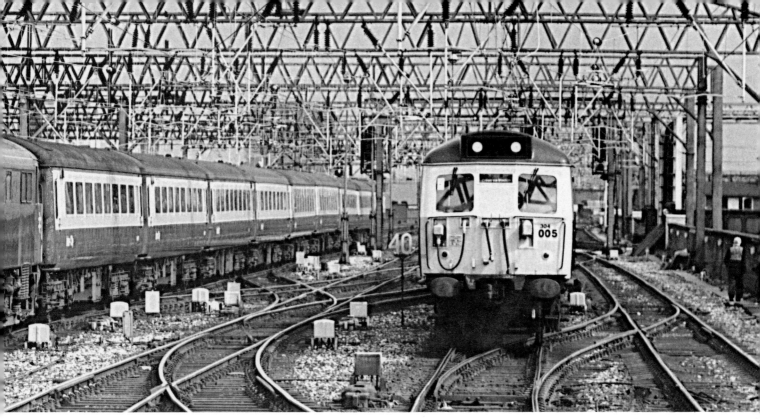

239.
A panoramic view of the approaches to Manchester Piccadilly station, with Class 86/2 No. 86243 *The Boys' Brigade* heading empty coaching stock from Longsight sidings and flanked on either side by emus. To the right, Class 304 No. 005 forms a service from Crewe with a Class 506 unit for Glossop, since withdrawn, on the left.

John S. Whiteley

241.
On 15th June 1984, a local service for Watford departs from Euston, formed of a Class 501 emu No. 501176 and passes three quite imminent express departures headed, from left to right, by Class 87/0s Nos 87027 *Wolf of Badenoch* and 87029 *Earl Marischal* and 86/2 No. 86236 *Josiah Wedgwood*. The Class 501 units have been withdrawn since this photograph was taken and replaced by new generation Class 313s and 317s.

Freight – Ancient and Modern

242.

At the time of this photograph being taken on 5th October 1965, pick-up freight trains could still be seen on BR metals, even utilising what was then the newest type of motive power. Having added some vans to the initial load that had emanated from Willesden, Type AL6 No. E3122 (now Class 86/4 No. 86412 *Elizabeth Garrett Anderson*), restarts the train from Watford Junction and heads northwards.

C.R. Lewis Coles

243.

Empty coal trucks are hauled northwards through Carpenders Park, on 1st July 1968 by Type AL6 No. E3182 (now Class 86/2 No. 86245 *Dudley Castle*).

Rev. Graham Wise

244.
Class 87 No. 87021, which now carries the name *Robert the Bruce,* heads a long rake of 'cartics' containing Ford motor cars and passes Bushey on 30th June 1976.

245.
On the same day, Class 83 No. 83006 emerges from the southern portal of Watford Tunnel with a mixed load that includes a bogie tank and 4-wheel fruit vans containing bananas.

246.
A visit to Greenholme, near Shap, rewarded the photographer with this rare sight of a Class 86/2 hauling an unfitted freight. No. 86241 *Glenfiddich* heads south on 4th June 1979.

Colin J. Marsden

247.
Passing Hanslope Junction, north of Wolverton, Buckinghamshire on 29th October 1981, a long freight headed by five 'Polybulk' bogie hoppers moves south for Willesden on 29th October 1981 hauled by Class 83 No. 83005.

Michael J. Collins

248.
Class 86/0 No. 86016 (now 86416 *Wigan Pier*) passes Rugby station on 21st April 1979 hauling bogie tanks for Ripple Lane yard, Barking, Essex.

249.
Beneath a maze of catenary near Watford Junction on 12th May 1979, Class 85 No. 85010 heads northwards for Ince, Cheshire, with a block load of 'Shellstar' pallet vans carrying fertiliser.

Antony Guppy

250.
With a load that consists mainly of ferry wagons, a Bescot-Willesden Speedlink freight service passes through Birmingham International station on 31st January 1987, powered by Class 85 No. 85025.

251.
In ex-works condition, Class 84 No. 84010 races through Watford Junction station on 12th May 1979 heading an express parcels service for Euston.

Antony Guppy

252.
On 28th October 1981, Class 83 No. 83012 heads south near Wolverton with a well-laden Freightliner service bound for Southampton.

Michael J. Collins

253.
Despite carrying InterCity Sector livery, Class 87/0s Nos 87007 *City of Manchester* and 87006 *Glasgow Garden Festival* power a southbound haul of steel coil from Dee Marsh sidings, near Shotton, and are seen near Winsford, north of Crewe, on 9th December 1987.

Ken Brunt

254.
Passing through Blackrigg, north of Carlisle, on 8th June 1979, Class 85 No. 85016 has charge of a rake of down petrol tanks.

Colin J. Marsden

Works Attention

255.
The first ever AC electric locomotive to undergo a general repair at Stratford Major Depot in East London was No. 86228 *Vulcan Heritage*. Viewed from the overhead crane on 3rd February 1987, the locomotive has for company a Class 31, a Class 37 and three Class 47 diesels.

256.
Just over three weeks later, the second electric locomotive arrived at Stratford for 'Level 5' overhaul and the first of Class 87. Sheltering behind its own bogies on 27th February 1987 is No. 87021 *Robert the Bruce*.

257.
Inside the Crewe Works of BREL on 24th April 1987, Class 86/2 No. 86207 *City of Lichfield* undergoes repair alongside a Class 56 diesel, No. 56088 with two Class 87/0s to the rear, Nos 87026 *Sir Richard Arkwright* and 87029 *Earl Marischal* respectively. In May 1988, Crewe Works commenced the conversion of ten dedicated Freightliner Sector Class 86/2 locomotives to 86/5 by altering the gear ratios and permitting a top speed of only 75mph. At the time of writing, the first two so converted are Nos 86258 *Talyllyn* and 86222 *Lloyds List* which are now identified as Nos 86501 and 86502, respectively.

258.
A new sector livery introduced on InterCity 125 power cars as a part of 'InterCity 21' activities and standard for Class 90 and 91, was extended to embrace Class 86 and 87 from February 1988. In pristine condition, overhaul having just been completed at Stratford Major Depot on 2nd March 1988, Class 86/4 No. 86419 at least carries a reasonably sized TOPS number.

No Power of the
AC Electrics!

259.
Often, as a result of weekend line occupation by permanent way maintenance staff, it is necessary for train diversions to take place. Where these diversions utilise non-electrified lines it is necessary for electrically powered trains to receive diesel haulage until returning to the overhead lines once again. On 22nd July 1984, the 07.57 Wolverhampton-Euston service with Class 87/0 No. 87012 *Coeur de Lion* is dragged through Whitacre Junction, on the Birmingham-Nuneaton line, by Class 47/4 No. 47555 *The Commonwealth Spirit*.

John Tuffs

261.
Above: Another of the trains described in caption 136 that were hauled by Class 25s that have since been withdrawn from service, was the 10.00 Wolverhampton-Euston, with No. 25256 dragging Class 87/0 No. 87020 *North Briton* and nine bogies on the descent of Camden Bank on April Fools' Day 1984.

262.
Below: Before the North London line electrification was completed in 1988, it was necessary to utilise diesel haulage for the one electrically-powered passenger service that then used the part of the route from Stratford through to Willesden. On 24th October 1987, the "European", from Harwich Parkeston Quay to Edinburgh and Glasgow, and utilising Class 86/2 No. 86261 *Driver John Axon G.C.*, is dragged through Homerton, in East London, by Class 47/4 No. 47518.

260.
Below left: In Kenyon Cutting, near Newton-le-Willows on 1st June 1980, an eastbound train of Mk 1 stock with 'dead' Class 86/2 No. 86233 (now named *Laurence Olivier*) is hauled back to electrified lines by Class 47/3 No. 47314.

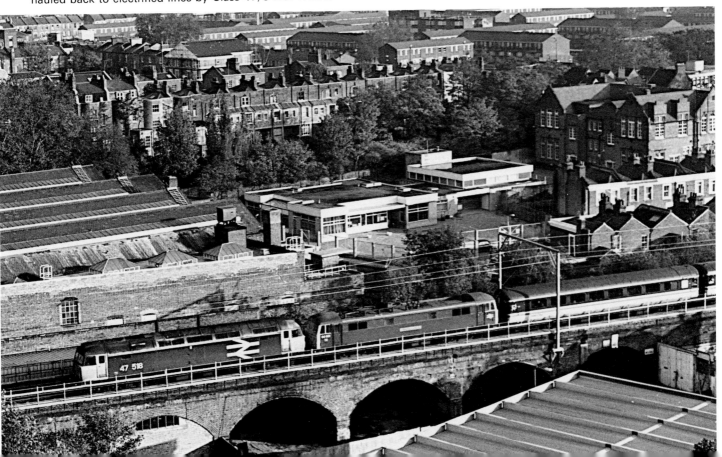

263.
Class 47/4 No. 47434 hauls Class 87/0 No. 87006 *City of Glasgow* and a diverted Glasgow Central-Euston express into Manchester
Victoria station on 29th August 1982, where a crew change is to take place.

Larry Goddard

Push and Pull

264, 265 & 266.

The BR Class 90 locomotives are designed to operate in similar 'push-pull' vein as the Scottish Region Edinburgh-Glasgow services, with 'Driving Van Trailers' (DVTs) styled to match. A total of 52 DVTs are being constructed by BREL for 'push-pull' operation on the West Coast Main Line and to obtain operating experience, temporary DVT conversions from InterCity 125 power cars have taken place with adapted Class 86/2 locomotives fitted for 'push-pull' and utilising 'Time Division Multiplex' equipment.

Above: One of the adapted Class 86/2s, No. 86228 *Vulcan Heritage,* attached to converted HST power car No. 43014 and a four-coach test train, is seen at Wembley InterCity Depot yards on 22nd November 1987.

Below: Running through Kenton on a test run from Wembley to Rugby on 20th November 1987, No. 86240 *Bishop Eric Treacy* provides the power with temporary DVT No. 43123 bringing up the rear.

Life Expired

267.
On Christmas Eve 1977 near the north end of Kensal Green Tunnel, Willesden, a collision occurred between Class 83 No. 83004 and Class 47 diesel locomotive No. 47163. As can be seen, damage to the electric locomotive was extremely severe and, after towing to Willesden depot on temporary bogies, it was formally withdrawn from service and cut up in February 1978. The Class 47 spent 19 months in Crewe Works before being returned to traffic.

Colin J. Marsden collection

268.
The number of new units and locomotives that have arrived on BR metals over the past few years must, of necessity, displace many older types from service. This factor is reflected in the large line-up of redundant locomotives seen on Stone Yard bank outside the Melts shop at BREL Crewe on 9th April 1987. Included are Classes 81, 84 and 85 locomotives Nos 81015, 84008 and 85001 in addition to examples of diesel traction with Classes 40, 45 and 47 to be seen.

Silhouettes

269.
Soon after sunset on an April day in 1986, a mixed freight train that includes 'cartics' travels north on the West Coast Main Line near Leighton Buzzard, hauled by Class 81 No. 81014 which was withdrawn from service some two years later in March 1988.

Ken Brunt

270.
Silhouetted against an autumn sunset, a Class 85 locomotive heads a down commuter service for Northampton near Cheddington on 26th October 1984.

Brian Beer

Glasgow – the End of the Line

271.
On 11th April 1982, the 17.30 service from Glasgow Central to Bristol Temple Meads passes Polmadie, on the outskirts of Scotland's capital city, powered by Class 86/2 No. 86238 *European Community*. The six coaches seen here will be augmented by a further six from Edinburgh when the trains merge at Carstairs.

Les Nixon

272.
The end of the line for West Coast electrification is Glasgow Central, from where an express service such as the "Royal Scot Limited", with just two stops, takes a little over five hours to reach London hauled by an AC electric locomotive, compared with a time of over seven hours for the same train in latter steam days. On 25th February 1985, empty coaching stock for Polmadie leaves Glasgow Central station hauled by Class 86/2 No. 86226 *Royal Mail Midlands,* which is painted in InterCity Sector livery.

Colin Boocock